Doncaster
Metropolitan Borough Council

DONCASTER LIBRARY AND INFORMATION SERVICES
www.doncaster.gov.uk

Please return/renew this item by the
last date shown.
Thank you for using your library.

InPress 0231 June 09

NATURAL BORN KILLER

NATURAL BORN KILLER

SANDY FAWKES

JOHN BLAKE

Published by John Blake Publishing Ltd,
3, Bramber Court, 2 Bramber Road,
London W14 9PB, England

www.blake.co.uk

First published in hardback in 2004

ISBN 1 84454 024 3

British Library Cataloguing-in-Publication Data:

A catalogue record for this book is available from the British Library.

Design by www.envydesign.co.uk

Printed in Great Britain by CPD Wales

1 3 5 7 9 10 8 6 4 2

Papers used by John Blake Publishing are natural, recyclable products
made from wood grown in sustainable forests. The manufacturing processes
conform to the environmental regulations of the country of origin.

Image on page vi reproduced by kind permission of Associated Press.
Every attempt has been made to contact the relevant copyright holders,
but some were unobtainable. We would be grateful if the appropriate
people could contact us.

To my children, Jo, Kate and Jamie,
who taught me love

Paul John Knowles arrives in handcuffs at Baldwin County Courthouse. Ron Angel is on Knowles's left.

contents
contents

PART ONE

DARYL GOLDEN

1:
7 November,
Atlanta,
Georgia

1:
7 November,
Atlanta,
Georgia

SANDY FAWKES ARRIVED IN ATLANTA, GEORGIA ON THE EVENING OF THURSDAY, 7 NOVEMBER, FLYING IN FROM WASHINGTON WHERE SHE HAD SPENT AN INTERESTING BUT FRUSTRATING DAY TRYING TO TRAP A FORMER VICE-PRESIDENT INTO GIVING HER AN INTERVIEW. She had found his hideaway office in Crofton, Maryland with the help of a friendly but teetotal Congressman's secretary. Crofton was a strange little place of newly-built Queen Anne houses, an upper-class Disneyland. The Vice-President's office was marked Pathlite and had no outside door handle. Sandy had knocked and made her polite request to no avail and had then retired to the local restaurant where she had been told he usually lunched.

He must have been dieting, that day. The bad luck that had

started in New York stayed at her heels like a faithful dog. Now she had been sent to Atlanta on an equally impossible assignment, but she didn't much care; travelling the world was what she loved most of all, particularly at someone else's expense.

Her stay in America was a super-jaunt provided by her temporary employer, an American weekly paper. In London, where she was a top reporter, it had been treated as a joke, but behind the laughter there was a certain amount of envy for the offer of a month's try-out had included travel, unlimited expenses and a generous salary.

The economic crisis in Britain had curtailed foreign trips for journalists, particularly to the States, and as, like most reporters, her curiosity was greater than her pride, door-stepping film stars or asking daft questions about flying saucers were a small price to pay in exchange for four weeks in America.

She checked in to the Holiday Inn in downtown Atlanta and was now sitting in her room. Its king-sized bed provided a heartless reminder that she was alone and, furthermore, randy. She wondered what to do with the evening. First she rang the local paper, the Atlanta Constitution, to ask if she could use their cuttings library, half hoping that her arrival in town would inspire some journalist to take her on a tour of his favourite hostelries. No such offer was made but the use of the library was hers.

She checked her appearance in the mirror. It wasn't worth changing out of the jersey cardigan suit she was wearing, but she tidied up her face and then stood irresolute in the middle of the room. She was dying for a drink, but printed notices scattered on every surface informed the customer that no alcohol could be served in the room. The thought of braving a bar in a strange city was unnerving; it was possible, too, that in the South they would refuse to serve a lone woman.

She sat in the armchair for a while, automatically reading the Gideon Bible that lay open on the table. The language, rich and strong, brought her childhood rushing back. Sandy was an orphan and had been left as an infant in the care of the State. After several years in an orphanage she had been sent to a foster-home. A bright child, she had not endeared herself to her foster-parents by being able to read at an earlier age than their own offspring and they had punished her by refusing to allow her to look at any of their own children's books or comics. They were delivered each week and left tantalizingly in the living-room, but she was forbidden to touch them. Not once in the four years she stayed there was this rule waived. Legally, she had to have a room of her own furnished with a Bible, so, lonely and miserable, she had read the adventures of the Old Testament for entertainment and had unwittingly acquired a heritage: a love of language that would later reach out and claim her for its own.

The brief passage to the past gave her strength; anything was better than sitting alone in her room. Remembered pain was just a short cut to self-pity. She gave her feet the command to take her to the bar.

She stood diffidently at the end of the darkened bar in the basement of the hotel, glad to see a jolly, bosomy barmaid coming to take her order. Scotch, water and no ice, she requested, using her grandest British accent so they wouldn't think she was a piece of stray off the street. Cautiously she looked over the top of her glass and appraised her drinking companions. The usual array of vast American men, mountains of flesh covered charmlessly in loud synthetic checks, a sea of open-neck shirts revealing grizzled hairy chests and obstinate necks. Sandy had observed exact replicas of these men in hotel lobbies all across the States. While they clutched that symbol of respectability, the briefcase, their groping eyes and leering smiles treated all women as broads, unless, of course, they were those sainted objects, their wife or their mother.

Mellowing gently over her second drink she listened to them joshing each other with amiable emptiness, heard the Southern greeting 'How yer doin'?', saw that behind the possessive family talk full of references to 'my boy' or 'my girl' lay the endless loneliness of the travelling salesman's life: hustling dollars all day, drinking with strangers all evening.

As her eyes became accustomed to the gloom she noticed the young man. His gaunt good looks made him stand out from the crowd, but it was the fact that he was wearing a tie, one that matched his flowery shirt, that attracted her attention. Smugly, she assumed he must be European, noting at the same time that he was chatting up one of the barmaids. Pity about that, she thought, as the scotch headed straight for her crutch.

While she finished her drink she thought of the phone call she had received earlier from Neil, one of the most consistent and amusing of her lovers; it would be good to see him on her return to London next week.

Sandy felt an odd flutter of discomfort but no surprise when she noticed the young man leave his place at the bar and walk towards her. Years of pulling in pubs and clubs had taught her that, despite being a bit broad in the beam and not exactly a raving beauty, she had a magnetism that drew men as if to a pile of iron filings. The flaming red hair helped. On her own territory she could have coped easily, but in these unfamiliar surroundings she was as nervous as a virgin teenager.

'Would you like to dance?' he asked, throwing her off balance even more. Jesus! Shades of the village hall. Even though she had grown up in jazz clubs and spent hours gyrating in discotheques, dancing was still something to do late at night when she had enough alcohol in her to dissolve her inhibitions; screwing came into the same category.

'Well, no, thank you,' she replied. Then catching the quick look of rejection on his face, she rushed on, 'I have only just arrived in town and haven't had a drink all day. I need a couple to wind down then I have to go to work.'

He looked a bit sceptical, but ordered her a drink and parked himself on the vacant stool beside her. She was embarrassed, not wanting the barmaid to think she had come in for a pick-up. She timed her explanation carefully for the moment when the girl delivered the drinks.

'I am a journalist, you see, and I have to go to the local paper for some information for the story I am working on.' She turned to the barmaid, who was smiling with indifferent friendliness. 'Excuse me, do you know where the Atlanta Constitution building is?'

The girl shook her head, then asked some of the other customers if they knew. Most of them were strangers, but one directed her up the hill. By then, she had privately decided on a cab, but noticed with satisfaction that the ploy had worked. She was established as a career woman at work and the young man looked suitably impressed.

'Will you be gone long? Will you come back? Are you staying here?'

Sandy had difficulty catching his words. His voice was deep and soft with an accent she could not place. But her smug assumption had been wrong. He was not European but American. As she leaned forward she noticed that he smelt delicious; her nostrils twitched, so did her interest. She swivelled round on her stool and took a closer look at what the bran tub of life had to offer this time.

Mmm, decidedly lucky dip, he really was very handsome; tall, well over six foot, broad-shouldered, narrow-hipped and as slender as a wraith. Facially he was somewhat Lincolnesque – towering forehead, jutting, carved cheek-bones, the nose a trifle beaked but narrow, and beneath the sparse, droopy moustache a well-formed mouth. The strong jawline ended in a firm, dimpled chin. It was a classically handsome face topped by hair the colour of scotch and water. But the skin was flawed, as though he had once had eczema. It was a condition she was familiar with, her eldest daughter had been tortured by it from birth and she thought she recognised in this man the same desperate anxiety to be liked.

She stood up to leave, her high heels making her almost as

tall as he, and smiling warmly promised to return in an hour or so. She was not at all sure that she would, but instant sincerity is part of the journalist's stock in trade.

The newspaper library turned out to be disappointing and the local journalists even more so. She visited the editorial floor which, with its orange and lemon walls and computer systems, was more like a design centre than a newspaper office. The antiseptic cleanliness gave her a sudden nostalgic longing for the *Daily Express* building at this time of night – the oily smell of ink permeating the stairs; the whole place throbbing from the printing presses; the benches littered with plates bearing the disgusting remnants of canteen food, grey peas and ketchup; exhausted journalists full of alcohol and anxiety. No one offered to show a colleague far from home around the town, so within an hour Sandy found herself alone in the back streets of Atlanta desperately looking for a cab. She was nervous. The streets were full of young blacks, arrogantly stylish in pop pith helmets. She had read enough about 'hate on the streets' not to want to be alone in the wrong part of town.

Safely back at the hotel she went straight to her room. What to do? Well, there was a brand new city outside and a brand new young man downstairs.

When Sandy Fawkes walked into the bar for the second time that Thursday night it no longer seemed alien; drink had done its job and the atmosphere was noisier and welcoming. She was relieved to see the young man still waiting, standing at the far end of the counter talking to an older man. He ordered her a drink – he even remembered no ice – and she began to relax.

'That trip was a total wash-out,' she informed them. 'I'm supposed to try and interview a local man who has just gone bankrupt to the tune of fifteen million dollars – some spending spree – but the paper has nothing on it; he must be a friend of the proprietor.'

'You from London?' said the older man.

'Yep,' she said, feeling more cheerful now she had the attention of two men, 'over here for four weeks to try to learn something about your country. All I've learned is that there is a hell of a lot to learn.'

Her gaze was directed at the older man but her concentration was elsewhere. To her astonishment the young man had slipped his arm around her waist before she had even touched her drink. Fucking hell, she thought, I've got a right hick here. This will not do. Using animated conversation and a nervous shifting from one foot to another, she deftly dislodged his hand. A cool look and he got the message, his hand stayed by his side.

But she followed him to the tiny dance-floor when he asked her. He was a spectacular dancer and she understood why he had been so anxious to get to the floor. His feet were fast, speeding with light from the buckles of his patent shoes. People stopped dancing to watch him, cleared the floor. When the music finished, a black man asked him where he had learned to dance like that. The compliment obviously thrilled him.

It was nearly midnight when Sandy realised she was ravenous. She had hardly eaten all day. The hotel kitchens were shut but the older man recommended a Polynesian restaurant a couple of blocks away. The young man insisted that he drive her there and as they walked to the parking lot in the cool night air she began to feel at ease with herself. There was nothing she liked more than an adventure, a day or an evening taking off of its own volition. She had long ago ceased to care about tomorrow, today was always today, whatever date it was given. Many years ago an old man, a friend of her ex-husband's, had told her with a twinkle in his eye, 'Remorse is better than regret.' It had been her maxim ever since.

He led her to a sleek white car. As she slid along the comfortable seat, she sniffed the newness of the interior and thought good-looking, good manners and rich. He may have to do.

The restaurant was dark, half-deserted and decorated with plastic palms. It is doubtful whether the natives would have recognised the odd mixture of noodles, fruit and chicken, but the lady behind the open cooker had a broad happy face, like a Gauguin painting and a plastic flower behind her ear. They settled in happily and drank steadily.

'Are you from around here?' she asked, realizing she knew nothing about her companion beyond the fact that he danced well and owned a smart car.

'No, I'm from New Mexico. My father owns a small chain of restaurants out there and I am his business manager. He is being sued for damages in the courts here tomorrow by a local woman, so I figured I'd drive across and keep an eye on things. The case is tomorrow afternoon.'

Oh Lord, a businessman. She groaned inwardly. Business was a closed book to her. Safer to stick to geography.

'Do you know, I don't even know where New Mexico is. How long has it taken to drive here?'

He drew her a little map to explain. 'I've been on the road about nine days. I stayed in Macon, near here, for a couple of days, seeing friends. But Texas is the big one. It takes three days to cross it. I never thought I would come to the end. But America is a great country. I know, because I have driven through almost every state. I never fly if I can drive. I like to see God's great creation.'

'Doesn't it get boring, driving hour after hour?' Boredom was high on Sandy's list of situations to avoid and discourses on God were right at the top of it. She could see that an earnest monologue on the magnificence of nature was inevitable unless she turned the conversation immediately. Hopefully she asked him which cities he had visited and out tumbled a stream of romantic names, New Orleans, Dallas, Houston, St Louis, Mississippi, Alabama, Kentucky, states and towns all jumbled up. She looked at her companion with new respect.

'And I am on my way to Miami now,' he finished. 'That's funny, I'm going to West Palm Beach tomorrow.'

'You should let me drive you there. It only takes a day and you could see something of the country. You never see anything flying over it all the time.'

It was worth considering. Apart from the apricot-leaved maple trees glimpsed from the train on her way to Yale University in Connecticut, she had seen nothing outside the cities, nothing of the America that is ignored by the media. To see it all with an American who was not journalist, politician or lawyer might give her the insight she desired.

There was a sudden burst of laughter from the next table. Looking up she saw that the man sitting next to her had broken his chopsticks in cheerful resignation. His hands had been built for shovels, not for the delicate transference of titbits from a bowl to his mouth. This was the America that had been missing from her journey, the real America with all its strength, vigour, ignorance, greed and hope.

She looked across the table at her companion. 'You are not eating,' she accused.

'I'm not really hungry since I met you.' He smiled to show it was a joke and went on sipping his Planter's Punch. She tensed immediately; he wasn't her style. There were some men who you could tell would be a good fuck and no bother; the mutual exchange of physical amenities would suit both parties and when the time came to split there would be only the warm memory of an amiable romp. This wasn't one of them. And, she admitted, it wasn't just his rather gauche sincerity or his youth. She had allowed herself a knowledgeable glance at his slender loins on the dance floor. The trousers were hairdresser tight and did not, alas, look as if they were hiding one of the great secrets of the universe.

Deciding that she could probably divert trouble with direct tactics, she leaned forward, smiling but shaking her head from side to side.

'Listen, I'm not going to bed with you. Oh, I know you haven't asked, but it sure ain't difficult to read your thoughts!' He seemed startled by her boldness, then laughed.

'It isn't that you aren't very attractive,' she went on, 'because you are, but on a purely practical level I have to get up in the morning and try to do this fucking awful job and then catch a plane to Florida. Much better for us just to have this meal and a dance and enjoy the evening.' She leaned back in her chair, tilted her head and tried hard to look scandalised.

'Besides, I can't go around screwing complete strangers. I don't, know anything about you, you could easily be another Boston Strangler for all I know!'

They both burst out laughing, but for once Sandy was shocked by her own behaviour; where on earth had such an extraordinary idea come from? The words had been formed without thought and she looked to see if she had offended him. His eyes were glittering with laughter, or was it excitement? Don't get too provocative, she warned herself.

'But the Boston Strangler is dead,' protested her friend.

'Yes, well, but you have some very funny people in your country, don't you? Look at that man who killed all those young boys earlier this year, and that nutty farmer in California who bumped off the farm labourers. We get to hear all about it in Britain, you know.'

She rose from the table to close the conversation. She made no attempt to pay her share of the bill; it would have offended the young man. In any case, he was using credit cards. Her good English manners, coupled with a sharp pinch of indifference, took her a few polite steps away from the transaction; she didn't watch him sign. Outside, the temperature had dropped and quickly he shed his jacket and wrapped it round her shoulders. It was a sweet gesture; she was vulnerable to sentiment and was touched enough to lean forward and kiss him full on the mouth. She drew back laughing, rubbing her face like a child. 'It's very bristly, your moustache. How long have you had it?'

'Only about five days. I had a fuller one then I shaved it off, then I decided to grow it again.'

'It will have to go,' she said firmly, only half aware of the unspoken promise in that statement.

When they reached the car her companion discovered he had locked the keys inside.

'I told you you were distracting me, now look what you made me do! I'll have to go back to the restaurant for a coat-hanger, come along.'

He didn't seem angry and the proprietor smiled indulgently at them, obviously thinking they were a couple. Something inside Sandy relaxed; it had been a long hard three weeks, travelling alone, sleeping alone, and here was someone who treated her as a woman, wanted to take care of her even if it was just for an evening. Why not enjoy the sensation?

He straightened the wire coat-hanger and slid it skilfully along the inside of the car door. There was a dull click and the door was unlocked.

'I hope you don't think I do this for a living,' he said, laughing. She was pleased to discover that he was a night person too and was anxious to stay out and drink and dance some more. He was staying at another Holiday Inn in Atlanta, so they visited the discotheque there and sat talking about music. When she told him she had once been married to a jazz musician, he said he had wanted to play the trumpet and guitar but his studies at business school had prevented him taking it seriously. Sandy still found it difficult to catch all he said. The noise of the music, the depth of his voice and the unfamiliar accent, added to the fact that half her mind was still planning a graceful escape, made concentration difficult. He wanted to dance only the fast numbers, so they drank steadily through the slow ones and somewhere during the early hours of the morning she conceded defeat and arrived at the 'why not?' stage. She had reached it often before. It was only one night of her life, went the argument, and people who didn't want the responsibility of a lasting relationship had to take their fucking where they found it. After all, you never knew how long you might have to wait for the next one.

He slid the car back into the parking lot of her Holiday Inn, turned off the ignition and lights, then reached over to the back seat, which was partly covered by clothes hanging from a rail. She looked to see what was in his hand. It was a small zippered case of brown mottled leather.

'What's that?' she said sharply, suddenly anxious. He grinned. 'It's my shaving gear.'

She understood at once. 'You aren't really going to do it?' 'Why not? We can't have your pretty face all sore.'

She unlocked the door to the hotel room nervously. What an odd situation to have got herself into. Fancy the elegant Ms Fawkes being railroaded into bed by a country boy.

While she pulled the curtains he went straight to the

bathroom, turned on all the lights and unpacked his shaving bag. She sat on the edge of the king-sized bed and removed her high-heeled shoes. Her ankles were a little puffy from flying all day and dancing all night and, while she was rubbing them gently, she watched him in the bathroom mirror. He had taken off his soft suede jacket, hanging it carefully over the back of the chair. Now she could appreciate to the full his magnificent shoulders. She had always been crazy about men's backs, loving the strength of shapely biceps and the deep valleys of the spine as the muscles undulated towards the coccyx.

He smiled at her in the mirror and began to apply the shaving cream to his face. Her eyes sparkled back at him. Now here was a man with style. She got off the bed and went to the bathroom. Without her shoes she had to stand on tiptoe to see over his shoulder. Absorbed as a child, she watched him remove the right side of the moustache – in two deft movements. When he had finished she handed him a towel and they both examined the result in the mirror.

'You look gorgeous,' she said. 'Far more handsome than before, and I don't think I have ever been so flattered in my life!'

'You can kiss me now,' he said imperiously and, obediently, she did, sliding her hands under his armpits, up his broad back, and over his shoulders; he was a beautiful shape.

She led him to the bed and began to unbutton his shirt, just the top two. She was skilled in undressing two people at once. She flicked open her top button with her left hand so that he would look at her bosom while she removed her tights. He watched her every movement as she hung them over the back of a chair. She moved towards him to kiss him again. By now, he had removed his shirt and the light caught the brilliant copper colour of his chest hair. His skin was smooth and tanned; she could feel by the texture that he was about 30. He was still wearing his trousers and, as her hands roved over his slender buttocks, and she gently gyrated her pelvis against him, her mind, that part at the back that never gave her rest from its own sense of humour, sent the message: definitely hairdresser's cock. Better keep lips locked and eyes closed.

Her dark brown, Christian Dior underwear had been bought to impress another but it was very erotic and, she was fairly sure, a cut above anything he was used to seeing, so she stepped out of her skirt and blouse so he could admire the view. Duly impressed, he turned her around to undo her bra; her breasts fell into his cupped hands. With her hands behind her back she found his zip and slowly wriggled him out of his pants. Speedily, she scrambled into bed while he disposed of his socks. Now, let's see whether he turns the light off, said the relentless voice at the back of her mind. Experience had taught her it was usually a decision decided by a man's confidence in his cock. He turned the lights off.

Getting into bed with a new man, exploring a new body, was a moment Sandy had discussed with women friends on many occasions. The kind of women who had many lovers always enjoyed a hot chat about men's performance in bed. It was often wicked but just as frequently a purely practical exchange of information. She recalled how a few years ago two girlfriends and herself had run a kind of Michelin Guide to

London's acting and writing contingent. Sandy, being newly out of the paragon-wife class, was inclined to bestow five-star status lavishly, but her singer friend had ruined the game one evening when she had donated some poor soul only 'P' for parking. They had all agreed that, whereas size may not be important in a long-term relationship, for a one-night stand it certainly was. It was at that moment when the palm slid down the groin, the very first nudge on the back of the hand, that you could tell whether it was going to be trick or treat.

There was no nudge. Not even a half-mast. Oh, Lord, this was going to be hard work. Blast, it was late and all she had wanted was to get laid.

She felt no resentment at his lack of response. It wasn't the first time it had happened to her; most of the men in her life drank too much. She had spent many an evening watching her love life disappearing down their throats.

'I can't make love in the dark,' she said, switching on the bedside light and smiling gently at him. He pulled her to him and the caressing and kissing began. Using all her skills, she worked him over with fingers and tongue trained to trace the response trail and from the first journey she could tell he was inexperienced. She had never minded being the boss in bed and decided that she might as well enjoy herself, so she took a swig from the bourbon bottle he had brought from the car and dribbled it gently over his genitals.

'That should give you a bit of life,' she said wickedly and they rolled about on the bed, giggling, sweating, struggling, slipping about, but never in. Finally, they gave up. Sitting astride him, she looked down at him as he lay apologetically against the pillows.

'Well,' she said, 'at least we have proved we are two genuine redheads.'

'I'm sorry, I don't know what's the matter with me.'

'It doesn't matter, it can't be helped. Anyhow, we have had a lot of fun this evening. I've enjoyed myself.'

She felt it was half her fault; she had been fairly mechanical in her love-making. She had been fighting off a longing for her lovely Neil, who could make her come at first touch, and she hadn't whole-heartedly wanted this man. She didn't-even know his name. He too seemed preoccupied; perhaps he was also thinking of someone else.

'Still, you did get me into bed, didn't you? Even after all those excuses of mine.' She held her head cheekily to one side. 'So you're not really another Boston Strangler after all.' She uttered a long, mock sigh. 'What a disappointment.'

2: 7 November, Milledgeville, Georgia

IN MILLEDGEVILLE, A SMALL TOWN NOT FAR FROM MACON, GEORGIA, ASSISTANT POLICE CHIEF CHARLES OSBORNE SAT AT HIS DESK ADDING THE LATEST PIECE OF INFORMATION TO HIS NEWEST CASE.

The file in front of him had been opened the day before, with an early morning call from one of the town's smart suburbs. There had been no problem finding the house as he turned into the street; the neighbours were clustered in small groups on the lawn.

The weather was already Thanksgiving crisp but Osborne felt a chill strike through him as he entered the house. The interior looked as if it had been attacked by a giant beast from a horror movie. Furniture had been overthrown and smashed on the floor; the mirrors were splintered in their frames; there were books scattered everywhere; the curtains and upholstery were slashed to ribbons.

This was the sight that had awaited Mrs Carr on her return from the night shift at the local hospital, where she was a nurse. She had called out to her husband, but the silence which greeted her was louder than the sound of the blood drumming in her ears as she made her way anxiously to the bedroom. There was her husband on the bed, naked, his hands tied behind his back, his body covered with blood.

Mandy, Mandy, oh my Mandy, was all she could think as she rushed to her daughter's bedroom.

Then there was a noise. It filled the house as she ran through it. It filled the street. It was Mrs Carr screaming.

The neighbours had called Osborne. They had heard nothing in the night. Having examined the bodies, the police doctor stated that Carswell Carr had been stabbed all over his body, but the cause of death seemed to be a heart attack. The weapon was probably a pair of scissors. The killer must have taken his time as the wounds were not very deep. It looked as though he had enjoyed tormenting his victim. Mandy Carr, aged fifteen, had been strangled with tremendous force, a knotted nylon stocking round her neck, another stuffed down her throat. She had also been raped, or at least rape had been attempted but there was no semen present. From the degree of rigor mortis in the bodies, the doctor estimated that the murders must have taken place somewhere between 11.30 pm, 5 November, and 3.00 am on the morning of the 6th.

A team of detectives set to work searching for clues. The

scissors were found, but they had been wiped clean of fingerprints, as had every surface in the house. In all that chaos there was not one print. The police discovered that Carr had last been seen in a local bar talking to a tall, young man. They knew the bar was frequented by homosexuals. No one had seen Carr leave or noticed when the young man had left.

Patiently, the police built up a list of items missing from the house. Most of Carswell Carr's wardrobe had been taken. Mrs Carr knew where he had bought the clothes and was able to identify copies of the shoes and outfits that had gone. They had photographed them and circulated their description. Mr Carr had been a snappy dresser.

Also missing were his papers, credit cards and the keys to the house. A brown mottled leather briefcase and a matching travelling shaving case had also gone. From Mandy's roomj a radio with a digital clock had been wrenched from the wall, from her wrist a transparent plastic watch.

The detectives were in agreement on one point. It was unlikely that one person could have done this amount of damage. They were looking for two people.

Charles Osborne filed the new piece of evidence.

Miss Helen Ray, a middle-aged shop assistant from the Zayre department store in Macon, had reported the sale of recording equipment and four blank tapes to a tall, red-haired young man. He had taken a long time choosing it, telling her that he needed one he could use in the car. He had paid for it with a credit card. The name on the card was Carswell Carr. The sale had been yesterday, she had seen the reports in the paper today and had remembered him. Her description of him was being circulated right now. Tall, about six foot, broad-shouldered, good-looking, with a Zapata moustache. The Macon police had an idea they knew who they were looking for.

3:
8 November, Atlanta, Georgia

THE DAY HAD BEGUN WITH A MOMENT OF PURE TERROR. She had woken in the darkened room, instantly aware of something around her, something so powerfully evil she was cold with sweat. She could feel an almost tangible presence on the far side of the bed, between her and the door. Later, she was to think of it as a tall column of power, dark and vibrant like the visible centre of a tornado, but at the time instinct had flung her stark naked to the door. As the light poured in from the balcony her fear dissolved like a child waking from a nightmare, and with it the disturbing memory of her companion's face in sleep, the lips drawn back over his teeth like an animal at bay.

Shaken, she cursed herself in no uncertain language. 'You stupid fucking cunt, fancy going to bed with a total stranger in

25

a strange town. You don't even know his name. You could have been bloody killed!'

Within seconds she was dressing, quietly, quickly. Pulling on her tights she looked at him in the mirror. He was sleeping like a babe. He looked harmless and at peace. Still, it had been a pretty daft thing to do, not much point to it either, as it had turned out, but she supposed she had better conduct the farewells gracefully.

She rang room service for breakfast and while she was waiting he woke up, a bit shy at finding her fully dressed as if it were a reproof of his failure. Having organised coffee, she became brisk. She had work to do and he would have to be on his way soon.

At 6 pm that evening, they were sitting opposite each other in the revolving cocktail lounge of the Atlanta Hyatt Regency Hotel and she was still trying to get away. It was like being in a maze, every time Sandy found an escape route he was there, blocking the exit. First she had failed to find a cab to take her to her interview, so he had driven her there. Then, after lunch, she had decided to make an early escape to the airport while he was at his court case. She was heading for the desk to leave him a polite note when he had appeared mysteriously, saying the whole thing had been settled out of court.

Still, one thing had been achieved. She had found out his name. It had been on the drive to the bankrupt multi-millionaire – who, as she predicted, had refused to discuss the matter. There was no tactful way of introducing the subject.

'Er, I know this sounds a bit odd in the circumstances but, um, I can't keep on just saying "you"... If you introduced yourself last night I didn't catch it. Your name that is.'

'Lester Daryl Golden,' he announced. He enunciated it carefully and loudly like a child on its first day at school. 'My family call me LD.'

'Why?'

'I don't know, they started it when I was a kid' and it just stuck, I suppose.'

How the hell can anyone go through life being called by their initials, she thought. Americans are weird. A picture came to her mind of a woman in a long apron coming round from the chicken house shouting, 'Elldee, time for your breakfast,' to a red-haired kid. Or did it have just one 'L'? And how the hell could you murmur 'LD' in someone's ear when you're coming? Should you ever get the chance, she reminded herself grimly, thinking of the useless wrestling of the night before. No, it wouldn't do.

'Would you mind if I called you Daryl? Daryl Golden is a beautiful name and it suits you, it's handsome.'

He was silent for a while and she thought perhaps she had upset him. She was always very annoyed when people called her Sandra; her manners must be slipping.

He nodded. 'Yes, I'd like that. I'd like you to call me Daryl.' So Daryl it was and he spent all morning trying to persuade her to drive with him to Florida, but her enthusiasm for a cross-country adventure was waning.

He was attentive and he was fun. They had stopped at an icecream parlour where she had peered in wonder at the selection, finally settling on a double butterscotch, walnut and pecan. She had paid as he had no cash. She had heard that Americans never carried money, only wads of credit cards, so she was not surprised. They had shared their treat in the car, dripping the icecream all over the black leather seats, as happy as kids let out of school.

But the uneasiness lingered. She felt as though a net were tightening around her. The sensation intensified when he greeted her after the court case. Looking incredibly glamorous in a custard-yellow, double-breasted blazer, he crossed the hotel lobby, smiling possessively.

'I've just rung the office, I have to be back tonight,' she blurted out defensively. 'I am booked on the 6.20 pm flight out tonight.'

He looked at his watch, a shabby affair for someone who always wore such chic clothes. 'It's only just after three and I've just saved my daddy a lot of dough. Let's go and celebrate, then I'll drive you to the airport.'

Relief had made her acquiescent. 'OK, I suppose I have a couple of hours to kill. Let's go and explore Atlanta, we haven't seen much of it. Why don't we walk? You see so much more of America if you walk,' she teased.

Now they were having a last drink together before she caught the plane. Beside her was a carrier bag containing the clothes she had bought at a shop in the Peachtree Center, a breathtakingly beautiful complex of steel and glass buildings reflecting one another, a kaleidoscope of lights and patterns.

Both Daryl and Sandy had been stunned by this unexpected vision as they turned the corner from the drab streets surrounding the hotel.

They had wandered hand in hand like tourists, talking of other cities. He told her of the superb architecture of Dallas and Houston, where he had often spent his weekends, and she was impressed by his knowledge of design. He had been a relaxed and comfortable audience, waiting while she dived in and out of dressing rooms. Between them they had chosen a pale pink satin blouse and a shirt patterned with an Erté design. She told him how she had met the great designer and had done a whole set of pictures on Bianca Jagger as a tribute for his 80th birthday. She tried not to sound as if she was showing off about her job, but she knew she was affirming her identity for her own benefit. America made her feel uncertain, insignificant; there was so much she didn't know; her insecurity was showing.

They had discovered the Hyatt Regency Hotel by accident, too. Daryl had said he had heard it was extraordinary inside and it was. A towering cavern, like an interior Garden of Babylon with fountains, wild birds, and plants trailing from balconies over 20 storeys high. Its awesome beauty was, almost inevitably, flawed by vulgarity. The elevators of black and gold and glass, designed to resemble hot air balloons and rising at an intestinal lurch of 700 feet a minute, turned an architect's dream into a toytown nightmare.

At the top was the revolving Polaris bar, circular, blue glass with a dome and views across the whole of Atlanta and out to Georgia beyond. Darkness was descending, the horizon was marked only by faintly twinkling lights; below them was a giant crane and microdot men working by floodlight.

Daryl ordered the drinks – Planter's Punch and whisky sour – and looked out pensively at the slowly passing landscape.

'And to think some people don't believe in God,' he murmured, his voice aspiring to poetic melancholy.

Sandy's nostrils twitched. Homespun philosophy was also high on her list of topics leading to instant boredom. Tartly she pointed out: 'If you are referring to the view, its beauty is manmade, not ordained by Himself.'

'You don't understand, Sandy. What I mean is that each one of those men working down there is making a contribution; every man who has ever helped to build something has left a mark on life. To leave a mark on life, that must be part of man's ambition, to be remembered for something...'

His deep voice rumbled on about how important it was to do something with one's life. It was almost as though he was talking to himself. Sandy couldn't catch it all; not that she was concentrating hard; she was thinking how sad it was that someone so ordinary should have such an unattainable ambition. In London, she spent her life among famous people, both professionally and as personal friends; she could tune in to talent instinctively and knew it was missing in the man sitting opposite. Somehow the vastness of the land around them emphasised the hopelessness of one human being trying to be outstanding in this country. Looking across the table, she felt tender, sad for the young man whose only asset was his good looks, the kind that so often accompany a plain mind.

He looked up suddenly. 'Have you ever written a book?'

It was a ploy she ran into fairly frequently, usually from men who hoped to trip her ego onto the mattress. She was about to air her number one excuse – 'I am far too busy living the next chapter' – when his next question floored her.

'Would you write a book about me?'

She groaned silently. How could anyone be that naive? Christ, he wasn't all that much to write home about, let alone a book on.

'You see, I haven't got long to live.' He was serious, scanning her face for a reaction.

'You what?'

'I haven't got long to live.'

'What do you mean, Daryl? How can you say that, how do you know?'

If this was his way of making himself interesting she wasn't going to buy it. No, no, that was unkind, if he was in the throes of some slow terminal disease the least she could do was offer him the comfort of her attention. Also, the calculating journalist in her was already alert. The slow fight against death had sold books before now.

'I am going to be killed. Soon. It might be in two days or two months, I don't know when, but within a year I shall be dead. I am going to be killed by someone.'

The change in the atmosphere was electric. The table seemed to shrink. There was nothing in the room except Daryl, his face intense, eerily lit by the candle in the red pineapple jar.

She felt the fear cut into her, as if a surgeon were taking a

31

scalpel and carefully removing the flesh from her vertebrae. This was preposterous, unreal. She struggled to hang on to her common sense. He spoke with a quiet certainty that compelled her to listen and she hunched forward on the table so as to miss nothing.

'I don't know who is going to kill me but it is for something I have done in the past. I can't tell anyone what it is but I have made some tapes so that, when it happens, the truth can be published. It will make world headlines.'

'Where are the tapes now?' she asked, not sure if she was humouring him or believing him.

'They are with my lawyer in Miami; that's where I am going this weekend. He has them in his safe and they are sealed with instructions that they are to be opened only after my death. I have made a will leaving the proceeds from the story to be divided between him and my parents. I'd like you to write the book.'

'But I don't know anything about you, or what you've done, how could I possibly agree? In any case, why don't you write the book?'

'The tapes are a sort of book, a diary with my thoughts about life and death.'

'And how do you feel about dying, that is if you are really going to?'

'It is fate. We can't avoid it. It's a punishment too.'

The waitress interrupted them to see if she could replenish their drinks and Sandy decided on a straight scotch this time. While they were waiting she tried to sort out her thoughts and sensations. After all, he could be just plain round the twist, or perhaps this whole thing was an elaborate joke at her expense. She looked at him intently but there was nothing to read, no fear, no anxiety and no twinkle saying 'Gotcha, you smart bitch.' She recognised that she was scared, scared of being conned on one level and scared that at any minute a stranger might walk in and gun him down there and then. Her too, maybe. They might think, he had told her his secret.

Once again her ignorance of America and its ways swept over her in a wave of panic. It was like being drunk at a respectable party where the heightened awareness makes one observe in detail other people's behaviour but the conversation is beyond one's grasp.

Her feet sent one message: get out now, your plane is waiting. The back of her neck was tingling with another: it's only a hunch but you could be sitting in front of the story of a lifetime. The hunch won. To walk away through fear would be cowardly. She would stay and, if there was no story, she would catch the 10.20 am flight.

The drinks arrived and she was all efficiency.

'Well, as you know by now, it's not often that I'm speechless... but what you have just said has absolutely astounded me. I just don't know what to make of it. I simply can't imagine anything you can have done that would make someone want to kill you. I mean is it something personal like an irate husband or lover?'

'No, I told you. I don't know who it will be. But it *is* going to happen.'

'Look, it isn't something that a fortune-teller or somebody like that has said, is it?'

'No, it's for something I have done.'

'Listen, I know you said you couldn't tell anyone but I have to keep guessing just to get my mind straight. Is it something to do with the Mafia, are you a hit-man on the run? Christ, that sounds corny doesn't it?'

He shook his head. 'It's nothing to do with the Mafia.'

'Well, the only other thing I can think of right now is that you must have done something really weird like break into Fort Knox... or perhaps you know the combination to the nuclear button and could blow us all sky high.'

She was floundering in an absurd montage of secret agent films and half-remembered headlines.

'It couldn't have been President Kennedy, too long ago, nor Bobby. Or are you planning to kill this one?'

That he was amused at her wild guessing did not escape her, her confusion and doubt were displayed clearly on her face. He smiled as he dismissed her ideas with a shake of his head and then, as if to demonstrate something patently obvious, lifted his hands above the table and spread the palms towards her.

For some reason she hadn't noticed them before but a chill like an electric shock shuddered through her as they glowed in the candle-light. The instant thought-association was *Rosemary's Baby*. The hands were like claws, vast and wrinkled. His immense fingers were wide at the base, narrow in the middle and as he turned them over she saw the huge flat spatulate nails like dead moons.

34

The thundering in her ears prevented her from hearing what he was saying, but she felt she was being pulled into his mind by those strange yellow eyes, flickering, cunning. like a fox peering from cover. The dark side of fear enveloped her. Against the highly sophisticated background of this spaceship bar hovering a quarter of a mile above the ground, she fought against that most primitive dread, black magic.

'Are you something to do with a cult, is that what you have done?' she whispered, remembering the satanic organisations of the West Coast and the mysterious disappearances of some of their associates.

He was too absorbed in what he was doing to notice that she was shaking. He was pointing out how the fate and life lines of his left hand formed a giant K. The configuration was repeated by the veins on the back of his right hand. Then he told her he had a small crown-shaped birthmark on his right shoulder. He had. She had seen it. Her mind dashed amongst the clues like a ferret in a gas-filled tunnel – Russian royalty or the second coming?

Either way, she had allowed herself to be well and truly trapped. The flight would leave without her.

'Well now, you aren't trying to tell me you are secretly a king, are you?' she said defensively.

He laughed and again she thought he might be scoring points off her.

'No, it's nothing to do with anything like that.'

'Thank Christ for that, I thought for a minute I was face-to-face with a real Jesus freak.' Her relief that they were laughing again was so genuine she didn't realise she had missed all the obvious warnings.

Sipping her scotch and inwardly giving thanks that she drank it without ice so her shaking had not been apparent, she examined the piece of information her mind had volunteered from its useless file.

Many years ago, at art school, there had been an amateur phrenologist, a man who believed you could tell a person's character from the bumps on his head or the shape of his hands. And fingers wide at the base denoted definite criminal tendencies. Then she remembered the same man telling her that her head showed she had no sense of humour, so she popped the information back in the useless file.

She felt very depressed. She was suddenly sick of being a foreigner in a land where the fact that the language was the same only served to emphasise her alienation. Every avenue she wanted to explore was blocked by her lack of knowledge; she didn't know even which questions to ask. This man was probably dropping clues all over the place, might even have explained what he was, but she had missed it. The very accent of America, let alone its geography and life-styles, defeated her. She felt a fool.

On the way out he carried her shopping and, as the nicely-brought-up image returned, the theatrical tension disappeared. 'You know, you really had me scared up there.'

He was both surprised and hurt. 'Not you? I thought you, a woman like you, would understand.'

Once again Sandy wondered what she had missed but decided to keep any future misgivings to herself.

They moved from the brittle glitter of the Hyatt Regency to the poorer streets of downtown Atlanta where several blacks were already lurching on the sidewalks, Friday-night wage-packets obviously well dipped into. They both looked into the bars half-filled with doleful blacks but lacked the courage to enter. Daryl, she noticed, was uneasy. 'Do you have many blacks in New Mexico?'

'Not a lot, mostly Mexicans, but I don't feel comfortable.' He shrugged the shoulders of his yellow blazer. He was right. He was out of place in this area. 'Let's go back to the hotel and change, then go somewhere special for dinner.'

It was years since she'd lived with anyone, so showering and changing with someone in the room was an odd sensation for Sandy. It was like playing a game of being lovers, being a partner in another's dream. There was a sexless intimacy about them, an ego-boosting conspiracy, as they helped each other choose their outfits for the evening. She wore her new satin blouse, split skirt, black tights and high heels and he was resplendent in a pine-green silk shirt with matching trousers, topped by a pine-green-and-white brocade steward's jacket. Having once been a fashion editor, it never occurred to her to wonder that her handsome escort was wearing clothes usually seen on male models. She merely thought he was exotic, rich, self-assured and that life in New Mexico must be very stylish.

The restaurant was as glamorous as the couple they made, with tall fountains, lush greenery, pink damask table linen and a full complement of cutlery. A welcome and civilized change from the single knife, fork and spoon on a plastic table-mat which seemed to be the greater American way to eat. The food was good too and, sensibly, he allowed her to choose the wine; no macho display here. The ambience worked. Sandy felt at home again and totally forgot her quest. If she noticed that he waited to see which knife and fork to use, she put it down to shyness or deference to her greater aplomb.

It was Friday evening, and the place was filled with happy groups and couples celebrating. Sandy and Daryl laughed themselves silly as the worst violinist in the world made his way from table to table playing requests; they played guessing games on which tune would be chosen and knew there was no way they could have him serenade them. Inevitably he bowed his way to their table.

'What would you like to hear, monsieur?' 'Ourselves, thank you.'

Very cool.

He was not so cool when the bill arrived. He seemed almost agitated, which was odd considering he had saved his daddy thousands of dollars that day. Perhaps Daddy was a hard taskmaster and mean with his money. Luckily, the restaurant maintained the European tradition of treating their customers like gentlemen and the anxious moment passed amid deferential bowing.

Back at the hotel, the barmaid greeted them like old friends and the evening was spent drinking and dancing in their usual flamboyant manner. The noise of the band made conversation impossible and all Sandy's professional intentions dissolved in a haze of well-being.

Very late, on their way back to their room, Daryl nudged her. Ahead of them were two men walking hand-in-hand.

Fully expecting a good bedding that night, Sandy was once again disappointed, though she had to admit that he did try. Every orifice in fact. A sequence of gymnastics that prompted the thought – not for the first time – that American men learn to make love from books; indeed, she could practically hear the rustle of the pages turning when they go up a bit, down a bit, left a bit. They know all the Latin names for genitals but lack that wonderful driving lust that comes from British men still thinking that sex is rude.

She managed to come by using the muscles she had trained in fitness classes,. Her developing self-awareness had been the result of overhearing cheerfully coarse chat among elite East End actors – 'like throwing a banana up Regent Street' was their description of a lady endowed with a cathedral-sized cunt and Sandy had taken care of her intimate muscle tone ever since.

Even so, it had been difficult to concentrate. No lady likes to be reminded of her age in bed and a couple of times in the half light his golden hair and lean youthful looks had reminded her of her seventeen-year-old son; definitely time to shut the eyes again. This, she told the back of her mind, is not the moment for a spell of pertinent self-analysis. I am perfectly aware that my penchant for young men that has developed over the last 18 months has subliminal Oedipal undertones, but this is neither the time nor the place for corrective training.

Her mind, however, was determined to put in overtime. While she was trying to turn Daryl's cock from blushing pink to purple proud, the processor was doing its own calculations: the exquisite clothes, the self-obsession, the finicky polishing of the shoes and self-adulatory dancing that needed neither the touch nor the look of anyone else.

She sat up sharply. 'Are you a homosexual?'

The silence was ominous. She regretted the remark immediately and pulled back, afraid he was going to hit her. It was a fear that had its grounding in experience; she had once had a lover who drank himself into impotency and had blacked both her eyes to express the terrible rage within him.

'You shouldn't ask questions like that, not now, just give me time and everything will be alright.' He sounded near to tears and she took him in her arms: 'I'm sorry. I'm truly sorry. It was an awful thing to say but it is better to be honest in bed. If you can't make it, you can't. Maybe you are in love with someone back home; there could be lots of reasons but don't let them worry you. It's probably sheer fear of this monstrous lady from London tackling you like a whole field of footballers, no wonder you want to protect your vitals, my darling.' She was aware that she was prattling, once again trying to talk herself out of a tight corner.

She reached out and lit him another of his Kool cigarettes and, while he smoked in silence, she tried to change the subject. 'Let's forget about it and just talk instead. Tell me some more about these mysterious tapes.' He didn't reply, so she tried another tack. 'I must say I'm glad we got back safely. I keep having visions of the St Valentine's Day massacre all over again. Do you know the person who is going to kill you, will you recognise them as they come through the door? I can't believe I am actually having this conversation you know... do *they* know what you have done?'

'They'll know.'

Feeling more and more like Mata Hari she chattered on, hoping to provoke some real information from him. One firm lead would do, a name, a town, or a date and she could be on the phone to London for reference in the morning.

'I don't see why you are so sure you must die. Can't you try and escape? You look very much alive to me.' She grinned. 'Well, almost very much alive, certainly healthy. Are you sure it isn't a morbid obsession? Have you seen a psychiatrist?'

At last he smiled at her: 'I saw one once. He told me I had the perfect criminal mind.'

Ah. There were only two uses for the perfect criminal mind. One was to be a super thief or gangster and the other was to use those same talents for government work. She had met a few villains in her time and they had had about them a cynical swagger, a pride in their anti-social status that was not part of Daryl's make-up. But then the role of a young business manager from New Mexico could be a very good cover.

'Was that when you were in training?'

'Sort of.'

He was certainly well-trained in the art of not giving too much away and obviously wasn't deceived by her belated attempts at questioning. She gave up.

'You aren't going to tell me anything, are you?' He shook his head.

'It's funny really. I can't imagine you doing anything awful enough to deserve being killed for... you like drinking and dancing and laughing too much, living in fact. In any case, I don't believe a word of it. I think it's just a come-on to get my interest.' She lifted her head grandly, pointed her nose in the air and sniffed. 'I don't think you're a maxi-murderer at all, more your mini-murderer.'

Making up her mind to catch the plane in the morning she clambered into bed and collapsed into sleep like the drunken babe she was.

4:
3 September, Lima, Ohio

ON THE EVENING OF 3 SEPTEMBER, WILLIAM V BATES STOPPED FOR A DRINK AT SCOTT'S INN, A POPULAR ROADSIDE BAR AND RESTAURANT FOUR MILES NORTH OF LIMA, OHIO ON INTERSTATE ROUTE 75. Aged 32, an account executive for the Ohio Power Company, Bates was a well-known Lima resident: His hobby was hunting and most weekends he would drive out into the woods with his guns and a sleeping-bag. On his hunting expeditions he liked to sleep under the stars. It was a Tuesday, but Bates still hadn't unpacked his sleeping-bag and guns from the previous weekend.

The barman asked Bates how his new car was running and the conversation was taken up by a young man who was drinking alone. Shortly before midnight Bates and the young man left the inn together.

Next morning Mrs Bates reported her husband missing.

The police traced Bates's movements as far as Scott's Inn. There the trail died out. William Bates officially became a missing person. His car, a white Chevrolet Impala, was also missing.

It seemed unlikely that Bates had joined the thousands of men who each year in America leave their families and simply disappear, but there was nothing to suggest otherwise. Except for one thing. Near the inn, the police discovered an abandoned car. It was a white Dodge and its licence number was traced to a Mrs Alice Curtis in Jacksonville Beach, Florida.

Mrs Alice Curtis was unable to reclaim her car. A retired schoolteacher of 65, she had been choked to death by an intruder on 27 July. He had stolen a few dollars from her purse and driven off in her car.

5: 9 November, Atlanta, Georgia

AT 8.30 AM ON SATURDAY, 9 NOVEMBER, SANDY WAS STANDING BESIDE THE LARGE WHITE CHEVROLET IMPALA – CUSTOM-BUILT AS DARYL HAD PROUDLY INFORMED HER – WAITING FOR HIM TO BRING OUT THE LUGGAGE. They were leaving Atlanta at last.

It was a damp, cheerless morning and her spirits matched the weather. Instinctively she knew she was making a mistake. They were going on this journey because *he* wanted it. She had been out-manoeuvred, a new and unpleasant sensation for a woman who was used to getting her own way.

She was shivering as he came round the car to open the door for her. As Daryl slid into the driver's seat, she glanced idly at the local paper he had bought her. The front page was splashed

45

with pictures and the story of several local murders. Earlier that week, a man had been savagely stabbed and his 15-year-old daughter raped and strangled. The police were working on the theory that these killings could be connected with several others that had occurred recently in the Macon, Georgia area. Crime and violence held little interest for Sandy and she turned the page indifferently, too hungover to care.

'Do you mind if I tear a piece from your paper?' he asked.

'No, sure, go ahead.' She handed it to him absent-mindedly and watched him tear out the top half of the front page: the story of the five murders.

'That's funny.' She looked at him questioningly. 'I thought it was only journalists who kept things from papers.'

'I have some friends who live near where it happened.' He was smiling, a crooked, semi-secretive smile, as he slid the cutting into his mottled-brown leather briefcase.

'Where is Macon?' Automatically, she gave the place its French pronunciation.

'Make-on,' he corrected her. 'It's about 70 miles from here and Milledgeville, where the murdered man and his daughter lived, is a few miles over. We'll pass quite near them on our way to Florida.'

'Mmm, nasty. I don't like horrible things like that, too morbid.' She pulled her coat closer against the early morning chill.

Leaving the parking lot of the hotel, he steered the car towards the road that led south out of Atlanta. As they set off, Sandy looked at the clock and sighed. Had she shown any willpower or sense she could have been on her way to the airport to catch the 10.20 am flight to West Palm Beach and could have been drinking with her friends beside the pool by lunchtime.

When Sandy woke from dozing, Atlanta was already 40 miles behind them. It was just after 10.00 am and the thin autumn sunlight was breaking through, the patches of sky a pale, clear blue. The wide road was bordered with stunted trees and grass exhausted by the summer. Stretching, she turned to her driver. 'Oh dear, have I been snoring?'

He took his eyes off the road for a second to look at her early-morning face, crumpled and a bit puffy from sleep and last night's booze.

'No,' he said gently, adding teasingly, 'but I was just wondering if you remember what you said last night.'

She looked back at him, puzzled. She was fairly sure she hadn't proposed marriage; her body felt too bad-tempered to have been prompted into a declaration of undying love; what had she let herself in for now?

'What time last night?' she asked cautiously.

'When we were in bed. You said, "I don't think you are a maxi-murderer at all, more your mini-murderer." Don't you remember?'

'Good God, did I ? Christ, yes, I do vaguely remember. Oh dear, I'm awful when I'm pissed – drunk I mean. Must have been all that mystery earlier on. Come to that, I notice you still haven't told me anything. Anyhow, since I'm here and not having breakfast on the plane, I'd like to stop soon, I'm hungry.'

'Yes, ma'am.'

Keeping an eye open for a convenient Ramada Inn, Sandy promptly forgot the words that were to haunt her for a long time.

Back on Route 75, Sandy was in a much better temper after a satisfying breakfast of pancakes and syrup. She started to pay attention to the landscape. The Grand Canyon scenery she had been expecting was not forthcoming. Instead, the Georgia countryside was as gentle as an English watercolour, undulating woods splashing thin golds and reds, the fast-balding trees making fine traceries of deep purple against the pale sky.

Daryl pointed out that Macon, where his friends lived, near where the murders had occurred, was just a few miles over the hills. He told her it was a centre for pop music; Little Richard had been discovered in Macon, and the Allman – or was it the Osmond – Brothers came from there.

Quite suddenly, he asked if she would drive. He was sleepy. He pulled the car over to the right and she slid across to the driver's seat. She was nervous as she had only learned to drive on the right-hand side of the road on this trip, but she loved American cars and this big white Chevrolet Impala was more luxurious than anything she had ever handled. He didn't ask, so she forbore to mention that her driving licence was in Florida.

She was surprised when he stretched out on the wide front seat and settled his head in her lap, but relieved that he wouldn't be watching her driving. It seemed extraordinarily trusting of him and would have been even more so had he known that she had not driven in London for the past three years. Not since she had woken up one morning with a strange young man beside her and her car in a mangled heap outside her house in Hampstead. The things I have done in the name of cock would outstrip the things that Catholics have done in the name of God, she mused, not that this little number slumbering in my lap looks like contributing much to the embers of my old-age memories.

She glanced at Daryl, fast-asleep with his head in her lap, a position that brought back warm memories of the times she had had it off in cars, particularly a crazy time a couple of summers before when she had given some bloke in a silver sports car a blow job all the way along Knightsbridge. Anyone taking a bus ride that night got more than their money's-worth. And she a fashion editor of a national newspaper too. Wonderful, wicked days.

The car was a joy to handle and as she sailed past more sedate drivers she indulged in a favourite Snoopy fantasy... 'This is me, Sandy Fawkes, driving a great big beautiful car along a freeway in the United States. Isn't life full of marvellous surprises?'

Working on a newspaper had taught Sandy to enjoy to the full every hour of her life. There only today counted; yesterday with its mistakes and triumphs no longer existed. That and her several attempts at suicide. Painful memories of despair and shame stirred as the miles rolled by, but they were eased by the knowledge that she would never do it again. The last time she had come round after being pumped out, she had woken beside an old lady who was badly shocked and burned from trying to rescue her 11-year-old grandson from a fire. The child had died and although the old lady had said nothing, Sandy had felt her contempt for someone who would throw life away that easily. And on account of a man, too. No man was worth that and none had infiltrated her iron guard since.

She turned up the radio to drown such morbid thoughts and concentrated on the nasal moan of country music. They were well past Macon by the time Daryl stirred and, guiltily, she slowed down. She had noticed that he was a very careful driver, always watching out for speed cops in hiding.

'I haven't been very good while you were asleep, been going a lot faster than you do,' she declared. 'I decided that if you are going to bump me off I had better try to get to Florida first, as I'd prefer to be a sun-tanned corpse.'

Daryl struggled to a sitting position and grinned. He seemed to know her penchant for terrible jokes by now and merely said mildly that he would take over the wheel. As he eased himself into the driving seat she leaned back against the passenger door, pleased with herself and provocative.

'That'll teach you, all that chat about being a mass-murderer, trying to scare me. And in any case, how are you intending to do it? You aren't thinking of strangling me I hope... it's supposed to make people's eyes go red and their tongues stick out, and I'm far too vain for that. Of course, it is also supposed to give men a hard-on – it's quite well known for older queens to try it; unfortunately it doesn't always work and they kill themselves by mistake. Shocking isn't it?'

She knew she was being wicked, but why? What was making her talk like this? It was probably frustration, sexual of course, combined with the sense of being conned and a genuine longing to be sitting in the sun. After all, this time next week she would be boarding a plane to London.

'And definitely no guns, 'cos they leave a very nasty mess. If you do it through the heart, all the blood rushes from the mouth, at least according to all the latest westerns it does. And I certainly don't want to be shot through the head and have my beautiful, clever brains wasting all over the road. So that's two methods ruled out. And another thing; *not,* promise, *not* in a Holiday Inn. I am a tremendous snob and apart from this job I usually stay in the best hotels in the world. I have a lot of friends back home who consider me rather gala and they won't think a Holiday Inn is at all a chic place to depart from. Right now, is that all understood?'

Not for one second was she serious, but a close examination of the map spread before her had revealed that she was in for a long and tedious journey; it was up to her to provide the entertainment. Her somewhat monosyllabic companion might laugh at her outrageous jokes but he was contributing nothing. Once again she wondered why the hell she had agreed to drive instead of fly.

He reached out and pulled her to him. With one hand on the wheel and the other round her shoulders, the miles rolled past, and autumn moved south to summer.

'Look at that stuff hanging from the trees over there.' Startled, she looked across the six-lane highway to the tall straggling pines, their branches laden with what looked like seaweed.

'What is it?' she asked. 'It's really rather beautiful.'

'It's cotton moss. It may look beautiful but it's a killer; all those trees are dying. It's a sign of the South.'

Strange fruit hanging from the trees, she thought, remembering Billie Holiday's bitter dirge. Like mistletoe at Christmas, that symbol of love and kissing at the death of the year, parasites plucking life from the tree. Beautiful killers.

They both seemed to be absorbed in their own thoughts. She felt restless as she watched America unfold before her, a vast sprawling suburb and resentful, too, as she considered the fragile reason for her journey. After the flippant conversation about him being a maniac killer, Sandy thought she had noticed the merest shadow of irritation pass across Daryl's face and had decided to leave that joke alone. It could become a very tedious theme and it was preferable to be bored than boring.

There was something else too. The images of death it had conjured up were vivid, private and painful. Her daughter had been exactly 11 months and three days old when she had walked into the room and seen the tiny hand make one last flutter through the bars of the cot. It was 10.00 am and she had been late getting up, but Sarah was such a good baby; Sandy had heard the gentle cooings as the baby had jumped up and down in her coat and she had had a leisurely bath before giving Sarah her breakfast. When Sandy snatched her from her cot it was already too late. Sarah had died as mysteriously and suddenly as the other three thousand cot deaths that were reported yearly in Britain and for which doctors could offer no explanation.

All day she had sat in the small room overlooking the

carefully-tended garden, talking to the little dead object. Doctors, police, friends saw to the formalities but none of them had been able to penetrate her pain. It had happened on 1 April and they had listened to her saying, 'It's past 12.00 pm now, darling, April Fool is over, please come back, please come back,' until she had seen the purple blood clots forming and had realised that this beloved baby, her firstborn, her only relative, was going to rot in a tiny grave, never to return.

In the car, she lifted her hand to firm her cheeks, disconcerted that the pain could still reach out and claim her after all these years.

Hoping to divert her train of thought, she turned her attention to the man driving.

'You know, I am still puzzling over some of the things you told me yesterday. I remember you saying that you had been told you had the perfect criminal mind; were you in the Services or something?'

'Yeah, I was a paratrooper stationed in Germany. I did 19 drops.'

'Gosh, isn't that scary? It must be awful that first time when you look out of the plane door and know there is only one way to go.'

'You have a lot of training first.'

'Did you get to London at all when you were based in Europe?'

'No. Did you ever get to Berlin?'

'No, oddly enough it's one of the few big cities I haven't seen. I was going there this time last year, to visit a regiment for a feature, but I got sent to cover trouble in the Middle East instead.'

More images of death. Blackened tanks like rotting teeth askew, in the desert sand. The shock of seeing holes the size of saucers in the solid iron sides, the pattern of splattered hot metal chrysanthemum-shaped around them. The knowledge that inside had been four young lads not much older than her son.

It no longer mattered which side they had belonged to; each of these obscene, jauntily angled fortresses had been tombs for four mothers' sons. For the men of each side they were war losses, for the women they were life losses.

The sky was a bright, clear blue by the time they crossed the border from Georgia to Florida. Sandy looked in vain for a definitive signpost but the hoardings were all busy coercing the traveller to visit Disneyland, see White Springs Memorial or drink Florida Orange juice. Her voice was small and cautious as she made her enquiry.

'I thought you had state borderlines with coppers stopping you and things?'

'You thought what?'

'Well, as you know, I've never driven across the States before, but in all the old films they were always stopping someone for carrying a minor or booze across a state line.'

He burst out laughing, a high laugh for a man with such a deep voice.

'Is that true, Sandy, is that what you really thought? Wow, that is funny! How do you think the freeways would work if all the cars had to be stopped?'

She had to admit that on examination it was a daft idea, though she didn't think he needed to laugh that much.

However, his amusement had dispelled the sombre mood of the morning and the change of scenery was a signal for her to enjoy herself again. Puffball clouds were poised postcard-style above tall palm trees and rich foliage; she had a quite endearing young man for company; what more could a girl want on a Saturday morning in November? A drink, came the prompt and unsurprising answer.

Daryl was not averse to the idea himself and promised to stop at the next bar. While they drove, she turned to look back along the road. Mile after mile of nature imitating plastic; nothing moved; there was not even another car in sight. With anyone else she might have commented that it was a good place for an outdoor fuck, but a second look suggested that the thick, ripe foliage could be hiding some very nasty things like snakes or, worse still, horrible fat spiders.

The road curved gently and she commented: 'It's like a play by Jean-Paul Sartre, where hell is being trapped forever in what you thought you wanted.'

She could see the remark had him baffled. Too European in context, she assumed and pulled herself together. She was not here to show off her doubtful erudition, she was here to find out this young man's background so that when she was far away and the unlikely announcement of his demise came over the UPI wire she would be able to go modestly to the news editor and say: 'So it was all true. He told me there was something special in his past and to think I doubted him!' And before their enthralled eyes she would unfold this extraordinary tale.

A likely story.

'Daryl, tell me something about yourself. Tell me about your family and the kind of life you lead in New Mexico. I haven't the faintest idea what it is like.'

'I guess it's pretty ordinary by your standards. I've got two sisters, my ma and pa.' He pronounced the words 'maw' and 'paw'. Sandy still had difficulty understanding everything he said. 'My two brothers are construction workers, they're both older than me.'

'Now what exactly does that mean, construction worker? Is that what I would call a builder? You have such different terminology in this country and I don't want to get it wrong.'

She tried to keep the irony out of her voice but he took his eyes off the road to give her a quick, suspicious smile.

'No, my eldest brother owns his own contracting business, the other one works for a big local firm but he's a supervisor... he doesn't mix cement or anything like that.'

'Sorry, but if I don't ask I don't find out. What do your sisters do?'

'My youngest sister is a beautician and my older sister is married.'

'Do you live at home?'

'No, none of us do. I don't really get on with my old man; we just don't see eye-to-eye. He doesn't like the way I won't settle down. My mother understands, she's a great lady.'

'Have you told any of them about the tapes?'

'No.'

Jesus Christ, this was going to be a great book. Each piece of information had to be panned for like gold, and nuggets such as

56

these weren't worth getting out of bed for – or indeed into bed, she thought cynically. If this was the mythical strong, silent type she wished he had kept to the prairies and while she recognised that being articulate was not necessarily a sign of high intelligence it certainly didn't make life easier if your interviewee was monosyllabic. There were no more disclosures so she fell back to speculating, trying to assemble some sense from the few facts in her possession.

How could someone from such an ordinary background have something to reveal that would shock the whole world? The only feasible possibility was that he was a spy, one of those quiet men the CIA train to infiltrate companies or organisations. Perhaps he had found out more than was good for him; perhaps the Secret Service were going to kill him. But really, the whole thing was too absurd, like one of those crummy movies they show on TV when sensible people are in bed.

'Why do you have a lawyer in Miami if you live in New Mexico?'

'My family used to live in Florida. I was born in Orlando, near Disneyland. We just kept the same lawyers.'

She noticed that he didn't tell her the lawyer's name. She was beginning to doubt the existence of both the lawyer and the tapes.

Daryl slowed the car down and drew over to the side of the road. Beside it ran a wide trough of thick, oozing mud, glossy emerald vegetation growing with unnatural vibrancy on either side. 'Do you know what that is?'

'Whatever it is it's repulsive; no, I don't know what it is.'

'It's the famous Swanee River from the song, you know the song?'

'Yes, of course I know it and "De Camptown Races". God, I can practically smell chalk-dust and rubbers at the mention of it.' Tentatively she started to sing. 'De Camptown racetrack five mile long, oh dee-doo-dah-day…' Daryl joined in and between them they sang songs from the schoolroom. Memories of Miss Turnbull, the perfect headmistress with grey hair and a bun, who had understood her and had quietly encouraged her into a scholarship at the local grammar school. Even so she kept quiet when the hoarding came into view announcing the 'Suwannee River'. Daryl had had enough advantage from her ignorance already; she wasn't going to tell him she hadn't realised it was spelt that way.

Repelled yet fascinated, Sandy gazed at the pitch-coloured marsh that ran like an open wound between the palms. Swamps had always filled her with fear; the first murder she had ever heard about had been a little girl found in a swamp. Soon after that, the family dog had died, his head stuck in the local bog. Her newly-acquired foster sisters had afterwards taken great delight in leading her to the park and forcing her to roll down the hill right to the edge of the swampy pond.

She had left the orphanage when she was four and a half. Her memories of it were hazy but depressing: nurses holding sheets over her head to make her sleep; being forced to wear different coloured knickers to show the other children she was a bed-wetter; the dread of the weekly communal bath that had left her with a permanent fear of deep water. An institutionalised child, she had been three-and-a-half years old before she recognised her name. Measles had rescued her from the bath torture and one night she and several other orphans were carted off in an ambulance. The man in the white coat had come towards her, a pencil and paper in his hand. 'Unity Boyce-Carmichele?' he had said and the older girl next to her had nudged her. 'That's *your* name.'

What an odd thing memory is, thought Sandy as she climbed back into the car and what an odd journey this is: constant echoes of death under a brilliant blue sky and waving palms. And in the curious intimacy and isolation provided by that eternal car journey she told her companion things she had thought were buried in her forever. Odder still, he seemed to understand.

6: 9 November Route 75, Florida

6: 9 November Route 75, Florida

'STOP, STOP!' SANDY SCREAMED, LUNGING FOR THE WHEEL. 'I'm sorry, really I am, I didn't mean it, forget everything I said.' At last he pulled off the freeway.

'That'll teach you to be so superior.'

She scrambled out of the car clutching her skirt, her hair. The wind was whipping across the flat land, the high afternoon sun barely warm against such competition. He came round to her side of the Chevrolet and grabbed her wrist.

'You thought I wasn't going to, didn't you? You thought we were going to drive for miles and miles, all the way to Miami without stopping, didn't you?'

He was grinning as he eased himself onto the stool at the darkened bar.

'A Bell's whisky and water, no ice, and a Planter's Punch.

'Jesus, you gave me a fright out there.' She was panting for breath. 'I thought you were going to drive right past! I promise you faithfully that from now on I will never say another word against Holiday Inns.'

Laughing, they raised their glasses to each other, swallowed their drinks at feverish speed and decided on another round. It was three hours since Sandy's body clock had sounded the alarm for a drink and during those hours the numbing perfection of the scenery had driven them both into long but not uncomfortable silences, broken occasionally by a question from her.

'How old are you, Daryl?' 'Thirty-three.'

Thirty-three. She was surprised that anyone could reach their 30s and be so inexperienced in bed. Still, she was quite relieved, at least he wasn't a whole generation younger than her; she wasn't cradle-snatching. About 18 months before she had cast a cool eye over the men near her age and realised that basically they had little to offer; the ones with the whisky paunches were hardly alluring and the ones who did look after themselves preferred to prove their virility with slender blonde 20-year-olds. She had stopped looking for potential living-in partners and discovered a new world full of entertaining, good-looking, vigorous young men who belonged to the unfaithful generation. She had grown up in the alcohol and monogamy group, standards which the young had cheerfully discarded; pot and unpossessiveness were their maxims. Pot she had never learned to smoke but she enjoyed the benefits of their other wisdoms. The last year had given her partners and a lot of laughter, glamour, fun without guilt, no responsibilities and usually no phone calls. Freedom plus a certain amount of loneliness: it was worth it.

'Have you ever been married?'

'No, I have been engaged a couple of times but it never worked out. I was going to marry a girl in San Francisco but she went back to her husband, and I was engaged to a girl in Macon but she married someone else. I know now I shan't ever marry.'

'How can you say that? You are young enough to meet someone and start a new life.'

'I told you, the reason is on the tapes.'

'Ah, yes, the famous tapes, it always comes back to them. When are you going to give me a hint what's on them? After all, I have more or less agreed to write the book.'

He hadn't answered at first, just gone on driving, looking straight ahead. She had had the oddest impression that he was two-dimensional, a cardboard cut-out, and that the piece of him she was seeing bore no relation to the real person he was hiding.

Then he had said: 'No, I can't tell you. It would be impossible for you as a journalist not to tell the story before it's time.'

'I wouldn't steal it, if that's what you mean and actually, for all that I talk so much, I'm very good at keeping my mouth shut.'

But he was not to be drawn and the barrier of silence had become stronger. It was not an uncomfortable silence; there was much about her own life she had no wish to share with him. Although she had mentioned her son, she felt a reluctance to tell him about her teenage daughters. In a relationship as ephemeral as a day's drive it was unnecessary to contribute too much of oneself. The thought of her family had made her homesick; her three kids, she loved them so much. They were a tight little family bound together by an intimacy that strangers envied. They had shared so much – being so broke that eating was an achievement, at other times throwing champagne parties for a hundred people. Probably too tight a family, she had thought. One of these days she would have to move away so they would have room to breathe, to expand and make lives for themselves. Besides, the girls were beginning to fancy the same blokes as she did and if anything could endanger their relationship that would be it.

Sandy was feeling decidedly better as they left Route 75 and turned onto Route 10 towards southern Florida. Her body wrapped comfortably around a few scotches, she looked forward to an evening's laughter with her colleagues. It crossed her mind that a couple of them would look a lot more attractive after the previous two nights' frustration. But contrition followed fast on the heels of such unkind thoughts. Daryl had really done his best to keep her happy. He was kind and considerate, laughed at her jokes, made her feel young and special. He had listened, engrossed, to the stories of her sad childhood. Why had she told him? Was it to prove she was different, or to show that she was as ordinary as he? To show that the sharp, well-travelled lady he was escorting was just as simple underneath as she suspected he was? It was difficult to tell, but there was condolence in his hard, dry hand and in turn she would be less demanding of his manhood, would offer him friendship and warmth in exchange. They were together.

'Shall we stop off at St Augustine?' he asked. 'It's not far out of our way and it's the oldest city in America.'

'What a good idea, I'm getting very fed up with the scenery. When you've seen one palm tree you've seen the fucking lot.'

On the map it didn't look too far away but by the time they arrived it was past 4.00 pm and the evening breeze was beginning to blow. It was good to see the sea again and better still to see buildings and people.

St Augustine is a festive place, filled with the contented hum of families enjoying themselves, meandering, scolding, eating, laughing, whining and dragging tiny feet: the essential sounds of holiday. The first landmark Daryl pointed out was the jail, the oldest in America, built by the Spaniards in the 16th century. Sandy's first impressions were delight at the old Spanish architecture and amazement at the scope of the vulgarity that had been imposed upon it. Everything was adorned with placards announcing the cheapest and the best, hot-dogs, popcorn, donuts, ice-creams, tacos, pizzas; if you could put it in your mouth on the street, they had it. It was the first time she had seen the great make-a-buck-every-minute-you-can mentality at close quarters; the very clothes people wore sang dollars. It was the consumer society with a vengeance. America.

She noticed that Daryl knew his way around the streets and he told her that his mother used to take him there as a child, as a special treat. He wanted her to see the old fort and was particularly anxious to find the torture chamber. She'd seen enough reincarnated pain at the Chamber of Horrors in London, but she followed him all the same.

He had no money for the entrance fee. It was only two quarters. It seemed extraordinary to her that you could buy anything thing from gas to a Cadillac on the promise of a credit card, but the system broke down for a quarter. Once again Sandy paid up cheerfully. Hand in hand, they wandered round the fortress. Discovering an arch half the height of a man, Daryl was convinced he had located the chamber. Pulling her reluctantly in, they found themselves in a high small room.

Her relief was triumphant when they discovered it was the gunpowder room. 'I hate anything to do with violence, one man getting pleasure out of hurting another,' she confessed. 'I identify with the victims too much, and feel their pain almost physically… just imagine being helpless in some sadistic bastard's power.' She shuddered and was grateful for the nearness of his shoulder. Daryl, however, was not put off so easily; the torture chamber he wanted to see and the torture chamber he was determined to find. He finally located it behind a barred doorway.

'I wonder what went on in there, what they did,' he murmured softly, speculatively, still holding her hand even though she was pulling slightly away.

'At least they were warm,' she said, pointing to a large fireplace in the corner. 'Which is more than I am. Anyway this was probably the guardroom.'

'That's maybe where they heated the branding irons,' he said with a wicked, teasing smile, but he took off his jacket and put it round her shoulders.

'You are a very nasty man,' she pronounced, 'but thank you.' They went outside to watch the cannon fired, a traditional and satisfactory' event that made them both jump and the children in the crowd scream with pleasure. Walking back to the car, Daryl called Sandy's attention to a group picnicking on the grass. A man was playing with his small child, swinging it by its arms, up and down, round and round until the child was dizzy. It staggered off, shrieking with laughter, then came back for more. Sandy watched the tender smile on her companion's face and felt once again that indefinable pity she had felt in the Polaris lounge. He seemed so ordinary and yet so lost, as if he knew that scene would never be his, he could not join, would always be separate. What was it?

The wind almost carried his words away but she caught their sadness. 'It's good to see a father loving his child. Men do love their children, but you have to be married to have children.'

Mine didn't think so, thought Sandy snappily, but for once she held her tongue. 'You are young. You can still get married and have children,' she said gently, knowing she was probing again.

'No, I can't. You know I can't. I told you.'

'The tapes?'

'The tapes.'

Sandy looked away quickly, not sure whether it was embarrassment or disbelief that made her do so. Why didn't she want to see his face? Because it would reveal the truth? It was enough to remind her that this was meant to be a fact-gathering trip and as they passed the ancient college she asked whether he had been to university.

'I took business and economics at Gainesville, not far from here:' Another short reply. She noted that all direct questions received only the most perfunctory of answers. Or were they clues?

'Not quite your style,' was Daryl's verdict of the roadside cafe where they stopped for an early dinner and indeed it wasn't, with its plastic tablecloths, trailer-size television booming the ball game and rows of boxing trophies, evidently the legacy of its lethargic owner's youth. But the fresh shrimps were delicious and they ate with the ravenous hunger of those newly-recovered from a hangover. It was dark when they returned to the car and Sandy felt despair in the pit of her stomach when he announced that he felt too tired to drive much further; could they stop overnight at Daytona Beach? Too exhausted to argue, she prepared herself for another evening with this enigmatic stranger.

Another roadside inn reached out and claimed them, the efficient and unquestioning haven for whose anonymity a million unmarried couplings give thanks. Unpacking for the fifth time in five days, Sandy found some stories from the newspaper she worked for, which Daryl seized, avidly reading her description of Ilie Nastase as 'rivetingly handsome, with olive-green eyes, a jaw like a Greek god and the most fantastic legs.' Sandy remembered with faint amusement the chagrin those words had caused her favourites and how every man in Fleet Street had wanted to show her their legs on the day of publication.

It was the earnestness with which Daryl said: 'I would like you to write like that about me some day,' that nearly did it for Sandy. The absurdity of comparing himself with the volatile star of the tennis circuit almost caused her to choke. Fortunately the British are trained not to laugh in another's face. Her inbuilt hypocrisy came to the rescue and, seizing the opportunity, she assured him she would, but he would have to give her the story. Could they sit down and do it now?

Feeling like a professional whore she walked across the room to him and put her arms on his shoulders. 'I will write something good about you because you are a nice man, handsome too, but you have to give me something to work on.'

He turned away and began to unpack his own things, hanging them carefully. 'Let's have some music,' he said and took out a combined electric clock and radio. The wires looked torn and there was no plug, but he made a makeshift connection and the digits flicked forward to the correct time.

They both thought of it at the same moment; what they needed was a drink. It did not occur to either of them that it should be anyone but Daryl who should fetch them. They had settled comfortably into their roles.

When Daryl returned, a drink in each hand, the setting was like a scene from *Psycho*. Sandy was framed behind the glazed shower door, the steam blurring her body. Daryl moved quietly across the room and slid the door open. She was smiling at him with happiness, with pleasure at being fresh and clean again, at his sweetness, at the drink in his hand. She leaned forward and gave him a drenched-face kiss, then took a sip from the polystyrene cup. Putting the drink down he came towards her again, carrying the huge bath towel. He wrapped her in it and tenderly patted her dry.

Lifting her off her feet he carried her to the bed, dropped to his knees and sank his tongue between her legs, his great hands stroking her still damp body with long sensual movements.

Well, thought Sandy, this is a bit more like it and she lay back in ecstasy, enjoying those wonderful moments when the nerves dart and the pelvic muscles begin to twitch then swirl of their own volition. But, of course, no one can keep their eyes shut forever when making love, it's too much like masturbating, which was exactly what her lover was doing when she peeped. So her eyes were once again closed when he suddenly shot into her with almighty force and held her so tight she thought she would break beneath him. But she kept him moving, rotating, grinding, until they rode gloriously together, her heart crowing with a sense of achievement. She had been able to give him something after all, and they lay together afterwards proud and happy, his maleness vindicated.

Later, while they were dressing, Daryl swore because he had not brought his clean underpants from the car. This time it was Sandy who volunteered to go and fetch them. Running to the car, quick of step and light of heart, she rummaged beneath the clothes rack looking for the shop-fresh pack he had told her would be there. Suddenly she didn't want to look any further; she was torn between the desire to please and an immense reluctance to delve into his belongings. She saw two sleeping bags in the back of the car and various articles of clothing that didn't seem to fit the man she knew. Odd pieces of junk too. She just wanted to get out. She slammed the door and ran back to the room. He looked at her strangely when she arrived but she paid no attention. She felt confused and embarrassed, as though she had been caught in someone's room, reading their letters.

'I couldn't find them, it was too dark.'

It didn't matter. He was already dressed, looking debonair in a black version of the clothes he had worn in Atlanta. The night outside matched their blackness and the car, now furnished with two chic people in high spirits, had lost its horror.

7:
9 November
Daytona Beach,
Florida

O N THE DANCE-FLOOR, HE WAS INCANDESCENT,
TOTALLY ALIVE. His feet glittered in the lovingly-
polished shoes, vibrated with miniscule, tap-dancing movements.
His slender hips were supple, subtle. His broad shoulders were
elegant perfection in the black brocade. And his eyes seemed
transfixed, mesmerised by his own feet. He was his own
creation, an animated animal electric with energy. Secretive, as
powerful as a flamenco dancer, he was performing for himself
alone, so strong and brilliant that the other couples drifted first
to the corners then to the shadowy room beyond.

The group and the girl singer responded. The music grew in
volume and tempo, inspiring Sandy too to dance as she hadn't
in years. It was marvellous to be alive in this strange land, to be

here: two people gyrating, together but never touching, on the shining yellow floor. Each was locked into a separate ego but coupled in the eyes of the world.

Later, settled in a darkened alcove, Sandy was grateful for the respite provided by a few slow numbers. She watched Daryl consume a vase-sized bowl of Planter's Punch and reckoned there would be no more thrills for her tonight. She had to lean forward to catch his words against the noise of the band. They were playing the Beatles' 'Yesterday'.

'...all my troubles seemed so far away, oh I believe in yesterday.' There was a wistful sadness on Daryl's face. 'You won't make me feel like that will you Sandy? Don't let me regret our yesterdays.'

As her hand went forward to clasp his, the word 'Judas' sprang unannounced into her mind. She had nothing to offer this man if he was falling in love with her, nothing beyond temporary companionship and sex.

With painful sincerity, he went on: 'I didn't know what to say last night when you asked me if I was homosexual. I didn't know whether to get all up-feathered or...' The rest of the sentence was lost in her outburst of laughter.

'Sorry, darling, but I've never heard that phrase before, where does it come from?' He grinned sheepishly and relaxed. 'Anyhow, you have proved me wrong and I hope you will do so again,' she added archly.

By the end of the evening, they were both silly-drunk and they took their glasses out to the seafront to clear their heads and lungs. The night was black and the sea lapped at their feet with an ominous purr; the swelling, undulating waves caught the reflection of the neon-lit strip behind them.

'It all began out there and that is where it will end,' Daryl murmured gloomily. 'Life came from the sea and the way the environment is going we will be living under it again in a few centuries' time.'

'Do you really think so? Honestly, the way you Americans have this amazing sense of built-in doom, no-one would realise that you are one of the richest nations on earth. You have all the ingredients for happiness in this life.'

'I think today has been the happiest day of my life.'

'I am glad to have been part of it, Daryl, very glad indeed.' She couldn't for the life of her see how driving a car several hundred miles made for a memorable day, but she kissed him warmly and together they teetered to the car.

Sunday morning was bright with early sunshine when they left Daytona Beach. They were both feeling jaded and conversation was sparse. Turning onto Route 1, which runs along the coast, they passed the nightclub strip. Sandy recalled the drive back to the hotel the night before.

'Your prediction nearly came true last night,' she informed him blithely. 'You were so drunk I had to drive. The road was so dark I nearly came off it twice. How would getting killed in a car accident affect your story?'

'It wouldn't make any difference; it's still all there on the tapes.'

'Ah... Why do you have sleeping bags in the car? I found them last night when I was looking for your pants.'

'Sometimes when I get tired I sleep out. Driving across Texas I fell asleep at the wheel. But only ever in the desert... I couldn't sleep in the woods.' He made an involuntary shudder as if a ghost had walked over his grave.

The sullen, grey Atlantic was on their left, the desultory flat North Florida landscape stretched to their right. There was little to interest the eye except a distant torrent of rain falling straight and solid out to sea. It provided a magnificent backcloth to the soul music and gospel songs pouring from the radio. The hymn-singing and exhortations to prayer were a welcome reminder to Sandy that she was in the Southern States, that the whole of America was not a set of plastic convenience units feeding the owners of more plastic units on wheels. They listened to the urgings of a black female gospeller and were sorry when the waveband faded.

'That's the only religion left that has any passion,' Sandy declared. 'You can really feel their joy, their sense of personal support from God.' She was throwing out another line. The journey was nearly over and she had found out practically nothing for her story. If there was a story, that is. So she had decided on a different tactic. If she could not get a clue to the contents of the tapes she had better concentrate on the philosophical background of their owner.

'I hate organised religion,' she offered, 'particularly the Catholic Church which must be responsible for more misery than anyone else in the history of the human race.'

'I believe in God,' Daryl complied willingly, 'but I've never been very interested in going to church. I believe in

76

predestination, fate. Man must do the things he must. He is alone. You cannot drive across America and see the great beauty it holds and not believe in God, but the biggest influence on my life was a book called *Jonathan Livingston Seagull*. Do you know it? It is about a seagull born white, with a higher intelligence than the rest of the flock and they cast it out because it is different. So it goes its own way, moves through life alone until it meets one other seagull, a female, who understands, then they go off together to create their own lifestyle and the flock watch and eventually realise they were wrong; he is a leader.'

'Yes, it must be very difficult to be an individual in a country this size. You have to fit into the standard image of success.'

'But he went his own way and he did find love, that's the important thing, love.'

Sandy fell to brooding about this mysterious, secretive traveller. What could have happened in the desert on the other side of the States that had isolated him from his fellow men? She could see no sign in his personality that he was as different as the white seagull, nothing that would make him an outlaw, a hunted man. He was too gentle and calm for violence. If he had enemies outside his own imagination it must be a group or gang affair. Maybe there were protection gangs in New Mexico. She was completely ignorant about these things and wished she had paid more attention to her student daughter's tales of the CIA. Jo would come home from the university with hair-raising tales of infiltration, dollars spent lavishly all over the world to overthrow legitimately elected governments, mysterious disappearances.

Sandy had dismissed them as the inevitable rantings of youthful wings beating for freedom and equality. Now she wished she had learned more from her daughter, whose interest in the history and literature of America was ardent enough for her to have earned her passage to San Francisco. She was there now. Daryl's voice cut across her thoughts.

'Listen to this tune and remember it. Listen to the words, they explain something about me.'

The song was by John Denver. 'Lady, sweet lady, this is as close as I can get...' It was a love song and Sandy only half-listened, hoping desperately that this was not going to lead to a sentimental declaration. The message was vaguely one of other commitments, of an incomplete offering of love. Sandy felt faint stirrings of resentment, as if she were guilty of asking too much from him. He looked at her questioningly at the end.

'Sorry, I drifted off in the middle, didn't hear it all, but if it was a timely warning not to get involved, don't worry, my possessive days are over. I find it easier now to spread my love amongst friends rather than concentrate it on one person.'

'I didn't mean to upset you, Sandy, just to say that I can't love truly. You are right, love binds people too much and if a man isn't free... I love my sisters and my mother is the greatest lady in the world.'

'Do you have many friends?'

His reply was cautious. 'I find it difficult to get close to many people.'

The impression was one of rejection, a history of failure to relate.

'Yet you find it easy to relax with me, don't you?'

'Yes, I'm happy with you,' and he smiled reassuringly, pulling her towards him so his arm rested comfortably round her shoulders. The miles passed by in companionable silence, broken only by his occasional request for her to light him another Kool.

Soon the signposts for Cape Canaveral appeared on the highway and on the spur of the moment they decided to visit it. Taking the long, narrow road across the causeway, Sandy sat up with excitement. Here was another adventure for the memory bank. The reality was a disappointment. Man's greatest adventure had been reduced to the level of Disneyland. The Kennedy Space Center was just another souvenir shop.

Remembering that she had not yet bought presents for friends, they toured the counters. Daryl helped her to select T-shirts for a girlfriend's sons, ballpoint pens decorated with moon shots for friends, keyrings, necklaces, bracelets. A cheap treasure trove carried carefully to the car by Daryl in a bright blue-and-white tote bag, the essence of an American experience as opposed to a European one.

Sitting happily in the car beside him, she chatted about her friends back home, especially about her closest friend, the mother of the sons. The number of times they had pounded on each other's door in the middle of the night, sobbing hysterically about the latest punch-up with their lovers, each disaster eternal until the morning when they would begin to laugh at each ludicrous scene until sheepishly they could accept responsibility. Although he laughed at her stories he had none of his own to contribute, no anecdotes that would illustrate his lifestyle back home.

Gradually the roadside furnished itself with dotty little houses, each tiny edifice the sum total of a lifetime's savings, pension pretentiousness with fretwork porches inhabited by respectable hard-working people whose final gesture was to clothe their worn-out, ill-kept bodies in brilliant, unbecoming bermuda shorts. When she had first arrived in Florida, Sandy had found the sight of ageing flesh, marbled like Roquefort cheese, bursting from amputated slacks, utterly revolting. Then its owners' enjoyment of life had communicated itself to her and she realised that they had earned domain over their own bodies, they had worked all their lives and were entitled to live their last years dressed to please themselves. It was certainly an improvement on the old Mediterranean tradition of putting peasant women into black from the age of 30.

Finally they reached her hotel in West Palm Beach. Although Miami was only another 90 miles' drive, once again Daryl seemed reluctant to move on. Sandy's anxiety returned. It was one thing to drive across country with a stranger, another to introduce him to her friends. It wasn't as if he had their easygoing, flamboyant charm. In any case, she was anxious to be back in their midst, to be flippant and free; she had already forgotten the point of the journey.

'I'm afraid you won't be able to stay with me,' she said crisply. 'My hotel room is being paid for by the paper and I'm sure they would not expect me to take in boarders. However, there is another hotel across the way, we can meet for a drink this evening.'

She got out of the car, praying that he wouldn't follow. She had her luggage with her. As she started to walk towards the hotel she felt the suitcases being taken from her. Daryl would not be shaken off that easily.

He carried the luggage to her room and waited while she changed her clothes. Her jeans, newly-laundered, had shrunk and her good humour was totally restored as he held them for her to struggle into. She protested that these were supposed to be private antics, but his laughter was gentle and full of admiration. Together they went to the bar to face her friends.

8: 10 November West Palm Beach, Florida

JOURNALISTS ARE AT BEST A MOTLEY LOT. Witty, morose, vain, jealous of their by-line or another's achievement; generous, greedy, competent, hardworking, lazy, the holders of a flawed talent. A million variables according to the job in hand, the group returning to now were all of these. Gathered from some of the best newspapers in the land, as well as many from London's Fleet Street, they came to Florida for a variety of reasons: a better living standard for their families, the opportunity for travel, the perennial sunshine, but mostly for money. Some of them stayed and learned, some stayed and became bitter, others failed and went home.

Sandy knew she would be welcome. She knew she would be welcome because she had failed, failed to live up to her reputation as one of the brightest women writers in Fleet

Street, failed to use her *Daily Express* connections to dupe famous people into talking to her, failed to achieve the interviews she had been sent to perform. She knew it and they knew it. She had been so sure of herself when she set off, now she understood their despair at working for a paper whose reputation had been built on scandalous gossip, even though its intention now was to improve its image.

Malice aside, they were still pleased to see her; her bawdy wit had enlivened many a dull bar and after perfunctory introductions of Daryl she was soon into a full-scale account of the New York gossip. She had warned Daryl to pay no attention to the barrage of badinage, and he seemed quite content to watch her in her element. Occasionally she put her hand on his arm so he wouldn't feel left out. Apart from a remark that they couldn't understand a fucking word he said, her escort was accepted into the small community without comment. There were more important adventures to be discussed, drunken tantrums to be relived, colleagues' characters to be dissected, all of which would be dutifully circulated on three continents by tomorrow. It was fun to be back. By the time the bar closed she had ceased to care that Daryl was still with her. She would get rid of him the following day.

He drove her to the office on Monday morning. Set in landscaped lawns that looked as if they were rolled up at night, surrounded by burgeoning hibiscus flowers and butterflies too weary with their own beauty to fly far off the ground, the newspaper office was sun-flooded, neat. The office was already in full swing; the executives were firmly in place behind their desks, working on next week's stories. Perhaps 'in full swing' was not quite the right description, for this newspaper was run on completely different lines to those Sandy was used to Here efficiency was everything. Talking, laughing, the exchange of jokes and witticisms were not encouraged. Concentration on the job was to be spread evenly, earnestly, throughout the day. Each job was jealously guarded and extremely well paid. The man in charge of the telephone bills gave a weekly lecture on the use and non-abuse of the telephone. He informed potential staff that if one number cropped up too often it would be queried, in case the offender was making private calls. Nevertheless, each story in the paper was checked by at least three members of the staff and the occasional willing interviewee could be driven to obscenities by having each of his statements verified by a different caller.

Drinking at lunchtime was not encouraged either and the steam-letting at 5.00 pm had on occasion led to incidents in the local bars. These were mostly verbal arguments that stopped short of physical violence because the ultimate disaster was being banned from the hostelries altogether. All information returned inevitably to the boss.

Sandy felt apologetic and rather guilty on the last Monday of her try-out. Her immediate boss had been kind and encouraging and she felt she had failed him. She had discovered last night that the jobs she had been sent on were the ones usually given to women who wanted to join the paper, but it hadn't made her feel any better. She had tried hard because she wanted to work in America, to learn its history, its politics, its people, but she knew she had not been a success.

The articles editor gave her one more chance. She was to drive to Miami the following day to interview the Attorney-General of the United States on the subject of the early parolees who were being put back on the streets before they had finished their prison sentences. The public were reported to be indignant at this development, saying that it led to an increase in violent crime. Sandy was pleased with the assignment; it meant another day out of that mental morgue and a chance to see Miami.

As she returned to her desk a young journalist, tall, blond, tanned, the image of the All-American boy, stopped her.

'Did you score?' he asked abruptly. 'While you were away?' She was astounded at his directness, then she heard a muffled laugh behind her. It was Mike Hoy, an Australian who worked on the *Daily Express,* also out here on a try-out.

'Did she score?' he hooted. 'She brought back a trophy!' Giggling like kids, Mike and Sandy arranged to have a drink immediately after work.

'Where did you find him?' was Mike's first question.

'Well, he shot me some line about some tapes and I got myself lumbered. He's supposed to be on his way to Miami to see his lawyer, but I think he likes our glamour too much to leave.'

'He looks like a redneck to me,' someone chipped in. 'A country boy from the South, you know, the kind of guy who lynches Negroes and doesn't trust long hair.' Sandy felt vaguely disturbed but put the remark down to jealousy. After all, she had turned down the men in the office for a stranger; you couldn't expect generosity as well.

Daryl was waiting for her at the hotel with the news that he had booked into the hotel opposite. Thank God, she thought, freedom. She told him she was travelling to Miami the next day and he promptly offered to drive her there. When she informed him of the subject of her interview, he replied smoothly that he knew something of the problem, there had been a lot in the papers lately, he would tell her about it on the way.

By 8.00 am on Tuesday morning the temperature was already in the 80s, a glorious day for a drive. Sandy and Daryl caught again the holiday atmosphere of the weekend. The sea to their left was a mosaic of reflections, the hotels and grand houses flaunted themselves in the sunshine, the air was full of the promise of the Florida season to come. This would be her last chance to get a suntan to take back home on Saturday.

'Are you going to see your lawyer today?'

'I'll ring him when I get there.'

'Perhaps I could meet him? Since I'm here it would be a good chance to make contact.'

'I'll ask him.'

It occurred to Sandy again that the lawyer might exist only in Daryl's imagination, but she applied herself to her day's work and asked about plea bargaining, bail bondsmen and the parole system, of which she knew nothing. Quietly and intelligently he explained to her that plea bargaining was a way of pleading guilty to the lesser charges with the assurance of a shorter sentence in a case full of loopholes where the criminal could be dicing with freedom or a 20-year sentence. That convicts were getting early parole because the prisons were now so overcrowded that the authorities were concerned about the detrimental effects of young offenders being thrown together with hardened criminals.

'Do you believe in rehabilitation, Daryl ?'

'I have no experience of it, but I do know that America is a very violent country.'

It seemed to Sandy that it was unlikely that she would be able to ask any very provocative questions of Saxbe. He was doing a television show and would have very little time for her. So she put the subject aside and suggested breakfast. They stopped at Delray Beach and on the menu was grits, something Sandy had read about but never tried. They arrived, a homogenous white puddle, flanking bright yellow eggs, the taste somewhere between rotting cardboard and glue.

'Do you mean to say people actually used to live on this muck? Jesus Christ, it's revolting!'

He laughed, covered his with salt and pepper and ate it with apparent relish.

They were passing Fort Lauderdale when Daryl said: 'I wish I had some cash on me, we could stay at the Fontainbleu.' Suddenly Sandy remembered her hairdresser talking about the place, saying it was the ultimate Miami experience; seeing that the paper was paying her expenses, she said there was no problem, she could pay. The hotel was easy to find: its massive curved front was swarming with rich travellers in bright checks.

At the desk Daryl gave her name, which started a confusion made more embarrassing by her handing over the money. She felt as if she were buying a gigolo. The knowing smile on the porter's face didn't help any more than did her fumbling in her purse for the tip. She was almost too annoyed with herself to enjoy the place, but the dark gold walls gleaming under chandeliers the size of radar-scanners soon soothed her ruffled pride. Their room was palatial, with two king-sized beds, a wall of mirrors and a huge balcony overlooking the sea. Room service was instant and they were soon on the balcony, drinks in hand, admiring the Olympic-sized pool.

'Let's go for a swim before my interview,' suggested Sandy, but Daryl had no swimsuit. This seemed rather odd as he had so many other clothes. As she dressed in a white halter-neck shirtdress and safari jacket, he fussed around her, straightening her hem, as attentive as a husband. Then he offered her his white belt which, to her chagrin, fitted her waist as neatly as it did his hips. Before they left she hesitated at the door.

'Look, if you haven't any cash I'd better give you some. I may be gone a long time and I find it embarrassing to pay for you.'

She gave him a hundred dollars but felt no better for it. There was a familiar ring of disaster about the whole thing. She had once kept a man for a year and the resentment it had caused between them was corrosive, destructive and only occasionally funny. It never occurred to her that Daryl might go to a bank.

The television show was to be filmed outdoors, an ordeal for which William B Saxbe was preparing beneath a pale blue plastic cape, the deft touch of the make-up girl removing shine and adding a tinge of health. Like any man caught in similar circumstances, he seemed a little embarrassed, explaining, 'Well, just flew in this morning, need a little something.' A big, barrel-chested man, at ease but as alert as his bodyguards, he expounded his belief that early paroling was responsible for the situation in America where in some areas people were virtually prisoners in their own homes after dark because of the violence on the streets.

Sandy thought privately that television was probably more responsible for the imprisonment of the American public, but it would not have been a good moment to say so. It was a sad interview from a man who had changed from being a hopeful liberal, believing in rehabilitation, to one who believed that the career criminal had no wish to change and was consequently better off behind bars. Sandy just listened and noted his replies; he had 25 years' experience, she none; it was his country. She thanked the television people for their co-operation and went to telephone her faithful driver; no reply from the room; no response from the bar. He was probably at his lawyer's. She called a cab.

Back in her room she wandered around aimlessly then slipped the chain-lock across the door, a habit she had acquired in New York and which the conversation that afternoon had revived. She rang the office, noticing as she did so that Daryl's briefcase was on the dressing-table. Would she try to get hold of Barbara Walters who was arriving in Miami tomorrow? It was almost as if they wanted to keep her out of sight. Still, it suited her perfectly. Another few days then back home to some real work.

The sky was dulling to lavender when the door rattled. As she opened it, Daryl's eyes went straight to the briefcase. Sandy noted his glance with faint indignation: the British simply do not go prying into other people's private property. Quite frankly it had never occurred to her. He had been in the bar watching for her to come through the entrance, he said. Well, he could turn right round as she was in need of a drink.

They didn't go down immediately, however. He wanted to change and ring his lawyer again. As he sat by the phone Sandy moved out of earshot onto the balcony. She could hear his deep, burry voice but was still not entirely convinced that there was anyone at the other end. Reprimanding herself for her nosiness, she gazed at the merging colours of the sand, the sea and the sky, only a distant twinkle defining the horizon. Below her, tennis players were enjoying the last of the light, their white clothes almost luminous in the dusk. Daryl joined her, fresh in a yellow silk shirt, black trousers polishing his white patent shoes.

'Do you play tennis?' she asked idly.

'No, I never took it up.'

Sandy was under the impression that all middle-class American boys swam and played tennis. There really was a great deal to learn. Nagging, too, at the back of her mind was the fact that he seemed uncomfortable in the surroundings of the big hotel, ill at ease in the expense-account crowd. Only in the car or in bars and discotheques was he relaxed; elsewhere his company was burdensome. An unpleasing association occurred to her. In London her smart homosexual friends frequently picked up young men – soldiers, sailors, workmen – in Soho pubs and bore them off to glamorous restaurants. Often an honoured member of these parties, she was aware of the boys' reaction: curiosity, awkwardness with the waiters, diffidence, their faces registering a history of fish-and-chip teas and a determination to remember every minute of the upmarket dinner.

She returned to her room to fetch her comb. Switching on the bedside light, she screamed. Daryl was beside her in a moment. A huge insect had flown at her and was slowly circling the room. Ducking her head, Sandy ran like a child to the bathroom. Once there, she had to peer through a crack in the door every so often to make sure he caught it. Her fear of insects and spiders had before now driven others to pretend they had caught the wretched things only to have them reappear later.

There was a gentle knock on the bathroom door. 'Look, it's only a hawk-moth, see how beautiful its wings are.' It was fluttering in his giant cupped hands, but Sandy had no eye for its beauty. To her all insects were alike. Repulsive. She slammed the door and screamed at him to get rid of it. When she opened it again she saw him silhouetted on the balcony, his hands outstretched, pushing the hawk-moth on its way to freedom.

She was still shuddering when she emerged from the bathroom. Her horror was deep-seated and genuine. Daryl crossed the room quickly.

'I didn't mean to frighten you, Sandy. It's just that its wings were like rainbows. I wouldn't hurt you.' Sandy shook herself for being so silly, gathered up her belongings and they set out to explore the night-life of Miami. The corridor and the lift were alive with visitors enjoying themselves. They spoke loudly to each other as if they were hard of hearing. You would not have thought they needed to invent the telephone, Sandy thought to herself, they could just stand on the hilltops and yell. Daryl caught her eye and grinned. He looked more relaxed now. Maybe it was the drinks or perhaps he just felt more comfortable at night.

As they crossed the reception area, Sandy was reminded of Italy where, six years earlier, she had first seen pink and yellow fabrics launched for men. At the time, watching the slender, languorous male models gliding along the catwalk clothed in soft pastels, she had written: 'Is the Latin lover a myth or a miss?' She had certainly not expected to run into similar fabrics draped over vast American males, all as masculine as bullfrogs. The women glittered with gold and diamonds and their bright-dyed hair was piled mountainously on their heads.At the exit they were stopped by one of Saxbe's bodyguards.

'How did the interview go?'

'Fine, thank you. Surely you don't have to guard him in a place like this? Excuse me, this is a friend of mine, Daryl Golden.' Daryl's face lit up with unexpected friendliness; they shook hands and the man turned to Sandy.

'Well, so many people come in and out, you never can tell. But we don't expect any trouble.'

'This lot certainly don't look like assassins,' she laughed, 'too busy swilling themselves.' The man caught the contempt in her voice and laughed too.

'Have a nice night,' he called, as they left the hotel. The

restaurant was crowded and people were queueing for food, something Sandy refused point-blank to do.

'We will sit at the bar,' she told the head waiter imperiously. 'Jesus Christ,' she said, turning to Daryl, 'fancy having all that money and standing in line to eat. They've got to be out of their minds!'

Sipping her scotch, she tried to explain her mood to herself. Was it envy of all that easy money that was making her so belligerent? Perhaps it was the uncouthness of its use. Certainly something was disturbing her. Daryl was quiet, sensing she was out of sorts.

Matters did not improve when they sat down to eat. The tables were cramped and set too close together. The plastic/wood tabletops did nothing to lower the decibel level of a roomful of Americans eating. Over the wine, her mood changed to one of appalled fascination, the vulgarity was so total, the obscenity of the food portions so disgraceful, the taste so synthetic that the evening took on the challenge of a walking essay in bad taste. The lady sitting on Daryl's right promised to be its high point.

Immaculately dressed in peacock silk to set off her polished walnut tan, her dark hair was teased into a perfect chignon. Her long fingers with blood-red nails were so laden with jewels, it was a wonder she could lift her fork to her mouth. She was also a master of the art of eating and talking at the same time. Not once during the course of the meal did she pause from her monologue. Her companion, who was sitting almost in Sandy's lap, uttered not a word. He was either a deaf-mute or mesmerised by the diamond-studded rattlesnake across the table. There was no way to avoid the woman's voice. It was a mixture of granite and rusted barbed wire, electronically-propelled, a corncrake would have been ashamed to compete.

'Well, I had to go to the jewellers this morning as this one was loose, I had to get it fixed, no, not that one, *this* one and she was there and she showed me this new ring he had given her, it was a 22-carat diamond and she showed it to me and really she shouldn't have. She hasn't got the fingers for it. I told her she shouldn't wear it, she hadn't got the fingers for it, she's got such small, stubby hands and it looked all wrong and I told her so, told her it looked all wrong on her hands... You have to have the fingers to wear diamonds, 22 carats looked all wrong on her hands, they're too small for a diamond that size. How can she wear a diamond like that on those hands...?'

The gigantic diamond – and the small, stubby hands – were the sole topics of conversation throughout the meal which, due to the speed of service, was mercifully brief. As their neighbours left, Sandy leaned forward confidentially to Daryl and whispered in mock horror, 'After that I understand why American men are willing to pay such large sums of alimony... I'd pay anything to get rid of a woman like that.' Daryl leaned forward even more confidentially, his whole face alight with amusement.

'I'd kill her.' Half-shocked, half-delighted, Sandy laughed loudly. They leaned back to enjoy a cruel and witty survey of the room, Although the restaurant was dark the queue had to shuffle past a doorway that revealed their shapes in silhouette:

haunches and paunches waiting to be serviced; monstrous outlines that could have lived for five months off their own fat; gross, sexless remnants of the fragile babes, the lean adolescents, they had once been. It was when the waitress offered them a doggy bag for the three different kinds of bread she had brought unasked to their table that Sandy finally gave vent to her anger.

'They should put the whole of fucking Miami in one big doggy bag, ship it out to Bangladesh and teach the inhabitants to become cannibals. It would solve two problems at once!'

After dinner Daryl wanted to see some white-haired singer who was famous locally, which gave them an hour or so to waste browsing in an arcade of shops in the Newport Hotel, trying on hats, riffling through souvenirs, buying postcards. At one kiosk Sandy spotted a mirror-faced watch on a clear plastic strap and decided to buy it for her daughter Kate back in London. She was about to pay for it when Daryl flashed the 20 dollars needed. To the girl behind the counter it looked as if she was being given a present and Sandy felt an overwhelming urge to announce that it was *her* cash, but she kept quiet. I really am a turd when it comes to money, she thought, without doubt, an absolute turd. She turned the watch on her wrist admiringly.

'It's so pretty I'll be reluctant to give it up.'

'I have a watch in the car you can have. I bought it for someone else but I'd rather give it to you.'

'Well... that's very sweet of you, thank you.'

They sat in a bar to write their cards and Daryl, who had a

sheet of ten-cent stamps on him, went out to post his, to his friends in Macon he said. On his return he took hold of her wrist and fastened a watch on it. She looked at it in total dismay; she had not been expecting a Cartier but this was decidedly not her style. It was a kid's fashion watch, the kind that had been very pop ten years before; now millions of copies had made it very passé. It felt uncomfortable on her wrist, didn't belong. She knew she would have to wear it all evening and, as gracefully as she could, she thanked him, telling him she would always remember him by it.

They watched the singer, a middle-aged man squeezed into satins and rhinestones, flanked by four pretty male neophytes, a kind of dancing Liberace. During the interval, one of those bright, pretty girls that America produces in abundance – big eyes, long legs, fresh make-up, teeth as regular as graded pearls – came over with a large camera.

'Would you and the lady like a picture, sir?'

Daryl turned to her, but Sandy's decision was instant and adamant. She knew what she looked like in snaps without the preparation of layers of make-up and careful lighting; even then the results could be disastrous. She had been known to come out looking like an elderly comedian playing a charlady, a Jewish momma at a barmitzvah, never like the face she arranged in the mirror. The answer was a definite no.

At the Castaways she insisted that he put her wallet in his shirt pocket. 'There are a lot of thieves in Miami, I don't like leaving my handbag around.' He chided her for being so untrusting but, led her to the dance-floor and they were off into their usual routine. Once again, watching him move, she began to find him attractive. They had laughed a lot that evening and he enjoyed life so much, helped make every event fun and, as she had determined that this would be their last evening together, she decided she might as well get the full benefit.

Back at the hotel, life was proceeding at full swing, mostly groups of males hailing each other as if lost in a fog. Sandy and Daryl thought they should make the most of their expensive home for the night and have one last drink. Sitting in the large drinking lounge, they watched idly as a customer came in, looked round, then sauntered up to a big man in an armchair. After a few words the two men left the room together.

'Homosexuals,' said Daryl, satisfaction in his voice, 'or "poofs" as you would call them.'

'How could you tell? They looked like respectable businessmen.'

'Lots of highly respectable businessmen in this country are gay. You'd never guess to look at them, all that back-slapping hides a lot.'

'Well, well, talk about living and learning. Anyhow, let's make all the straight ones jealous and go to bed.'

She was irritated when he went straight to the television in their room and downright fuming when he turned on a Swedish film with nubile young nudes cavorting on a beach. It wasn't as though he was the greatest screw in the world, but at 50 dollars a night, she was damned if she was going to be insulted by a bloke who preferred to watch TV. Furiously, she scrambled into bed, keeping her knickers on, a sure sign of displeasure.

'Aren't you going to watch the movie?'

'No I'm not... the last thing I want to see right now is nude girls, but if that's what you want, go ahead.'

'Aw, come on, Sandy. Just for a little while, it's fun.'

His answer was a humped shoulder with the blankets around its ears. Keeping the television on, he lay across the bed, trying to cuddle her into a good mood, but she had sulked her way to sleep before and she was fed up. Fed up with him, with the time she'd wasted with him, with the journey, with the effort she had made during this last month in the States, with the problems and difficulties facing her at home, with everything. Jesus, she was used to men who had an erection before they got her through the door! This was going to be the last time she fucked for a story.

When she awoke, he was in bed beside her. The television was still on. Balefully, she turned it off and clambered into the other bed. The next time it was morning and she sneaked out of bed without looking at him. Sleep had not dissipated her anger. She was at the foot of her bed, picking up her dress, when she caught sight of his face, the morning light full on it. His lips were drawn back over his teeth. It was hideous, fearsome, like a baying dog. Shaken, she dashed into the bathroom and dressed. When she returned to the bedroom to make up her face in the mirror at the foot of the bed his face was reflected smiling as sweetly as a child. The small innocent smile of a person at peace; the man who caught hawk-moths, who carried her bags and laughed at her jokes, was asleep.

Sandy went to the balcony with her notes from the Saxbe interview and settled down to work. Daryl appeared. She noticed that he never made a sound, she had not heard him get up or dressed, he always just appeared. He asked her if she would like breakfast and she said just orange juice and coffee. They talked in that strained way people do when they have quarrelled, politely asking each other their plans for the day. He was going to try to see his lawyer, she was going to sit with the phone and attempt to get hold of Barbara Walters' PR. If she could get her before the show they would be back in West Palm Beach that evening. Breakfast arrived and they courteously poured each other's coffee, his eyes anxiously on her, hers sliding away to avoid his.

A sudden gust of wind took the papers from her lap and within seconds they had disappeared beneath the partition that separated theirs from the next-door balcony. She leapt from her sun chair and peered over. The partition, built for privacy, was too high to climb over. There was nothing in the room which she could use to drag them near enough to grab from beneath. The space at the bottom was barely ten inches. She looked at him helplessly.

'That's my interview! Christ, don't say I've fucked this one up too!'

'I think I can get underneath. Don't worry, I'll get them.' Moving the chairs, he dropped flat on the floor and wriggled slowly under, his long left arm first, then his shoulder. His head turned sideways, grimacing like a Cheshire cat, then the upper half of his body disappeared. Supposing the neighbours saw him? They would call the management. Sandy grabbed a chair to keep look-out. He reached the papers and began the difficult slither back. Finally, he stood before her, grinning all over his face, and presented her with the papers.

'Oh, you are marvellous! Just like a limbo dancer! Oh, thank you !' Without her shoes on he had to bend down to kiss her.

'There,' he said, 'our first quarrel over.'

'What a bit of luck there wasn't anybody next door. Hey listen, if you had half the criminal mind you say you have, how come you didn't think of creeping under all the balconies? With the money they have here we could be rich.'

For the next hour she wrote and made phone calls, while he wrote letters. Once she saw an envelope with a green emblem and the word 'Macon' in the top left-hand corner. So he was used to decent hotels after all.

The sun started to blast its welcome way onto the balcony around 10.00 am and Sandy put her work aside and changed into her bikini. This would be her last taste of the luxury of hot sun until God knew when. Arranging herself luxuriantly on the lounger, she uncapped the sun lotion and wiped it abstractedly on her shoulders. Daryl, who was already stripped to the waist, came across and took the bottle from her hand. He sat at the foot of her chair and trickled the lotion into his palm. Slowly he massaged it in, first her left foot, right into her toes, up to her knees, all round her legs, behind the knees, then started again on her right foot. The long sensual movements stretched his body, displaying firm skin over hard muscles.

Sandy closed her eyes and lay back to enjoy the sun on her face while the firm hands sculpted her ankles, heels, knees. Even as the hands went over and under, round and up her buttocks and thighs she merely smiled to show she was enjoying his right to touch. Easing his way up the chair, he took her hands and smothered them in oil, parting and caressing each finger, the wrists, elbows and shoulders. There was something in the silence as he smoothed his way round her body, swooping powerfully, magnetically, that made Sandy lie still, acquiescent, while he anointed her with oil. Her eyes were open now, totally engaged in his. She watched as one great hand spread over her breasts, easing the oil beneath her bikini straps.

Upward went the hands, both in use now as he edged his way along the seat, blocking the sunlight, soothing, smoothing round her neck, the fingers seeking out each vertebra, the thumbs tracing the muscles of her neck, his eyes glowing bold, beseeching. The tension made her gulp, she could feel her throat agitating beneath his hands, but never did she feel a moment's fear, and as his hands slid away, down to her waist, she leaned forward and kissed him slowly, sensually. He eased himself on top of her and his hands were in her bikini pushing, searching and finding.

The Fontainbleu Hotel was built in a semi-circle and, with a prudish awareness that they might be overlooked, Sandy murmured gently that perhaps they'd better go inside.

'Don't bother with them,' he whispered into her ear.

'I can't, I can't, I won't be able to relax and I want you so much.'

For a moment he lay there kissing her, then he picked her up and carried her inside. Laying her on the bed, he spread her legs towards his tongue, leaving her helpless to contribute to the love-making. He still needed to masturbate to prepare himself for that one long plunge when he hit her nerves like an aching tooth. She noticed that he didn't come. The climax was entrance. There was no volcanic lava, that wonderful liquid heat when a man has truly shot his bolt, but he had given her pleasure and was satisfied.

The phone rang. It was the PR from the television company to say that Miss Walters was very sorry but her stay in Miami was so brief she would not have time to be interviewed. It was difficult to care but it was the signal for departure. They began to pack. Daryl tried his lawyer again while Sandy sat on the balcony, a post-coital despondency seeping into her soul. Her American journey was drawing to a close.

Looking back on the month's trip, at the places she had seen, she added up the pluses and minuses and decided that despite her failure to achieve her goal, a job in America, she had much to take home with her. The train journey through the autumn countryside to Yale and a Nobel prizewinner who wouldn't see her had given her the multicoloured maple trees. The drive to Princeton to the politician's daughter who wouldn't see her had given her a marvellous day out with an American Anglophile. He had bought her hot-dogs in New Jersey and dinner in Greenwich Village and had got so drunk he had fallen asleep before he could give her directions to his home. Finally she had abandoned him outside her hotel in his car.

In New York she had interviewed Lorna Luft and they had become immediate friends. Then there had been a crazy night in Georgetown, Washington with an ex-press attaché of Buckingham Palace and this odd week that had started in Atlanta. Not an altogether wasted month.

Daryl announced that his lawyer was unable to see him and that he might return the following day. Sandy went to the bathroom to collect her things. Unplugging her curling tongs, she absentmindedly picked them up by the wrong end and let out an almighty yell. She was burnt right across the fingers of her right hand. Daryl was with her instantly, pushing her hand under the tap, grabbing the ice bucket left from breakfast. Nothing helped, her fingers were as curled as her hair should be.

'I must have something to put on it. Please, please get me something to take away the pain!' He ran from the room while she kept her hand in the ice, taking it out gingerly every now and again to examine the great weals. It was excruciating. How the hell was she going to type with a burned hand? He was soon back with some yellow ointment which he spread tenderly on her wound, watching her face with concern while she clutched her wrist to ease the agony.

'Just give me five minutes and I'll be alright. I must sit down.' Deftly, quietly, his eyes seldom leaving her face, he finished her packing and called for the porter. Slowly the pain subsided and she stood up.

'Here,' he said, 'here is your money. I don't need it any more,' and he unloaded his top pocket and emptied it into her bag.

'Oh, I'd quite forgotten about it. Thank you, darling, and thank you for looking after me.' His concern on the journey was touching. The pain came and went in waves but gradually her fingers relaxed, became flexible, and soon she was enjoying the leisurely drive back. They stopped at a few head-shops and browsed amongst the jewellery, saddlebags and belts, the coke spoons and opium pipes. Later they had lunch and passed the place that served grits for breakfast.

Suddenly it was over. The holiday, the intimacy, were gone. An invisible curtain had come between them. Turning to him she said, 'The words will have to be spoken soon. I hate saying them but I'm going back to London on Saturday and I have a lot of work to do and people to see before I go. There will be no more time for us to be together... and you're not going to tell me the contents of the tapes, are you?' He shook his head, sadly but firmly. No, he was not.

'In that case I have to concentrate on my own business... but it's been a marvellous week, Daryl, wonderful, truly like a holiday. However, life must take over again. You have to go back to New Mexico. Maybe you will come to London one day, you never know, and then I will look after you as you have looked after me.'

'Couldn't we spend one more night together?'

'No, darling. No. Then you would spend another and I would have to leave you at the airport and I would hate that. Goodbyes are horrible but they're better over and done with.' He said nothing and drove on. She gazed at a landscape which had already become familiar – trees, houses, the causeway, bridges, the surface of the road itself – and as the journey drew to a close, she had a penetrating desire to be alone. As he pulled into the car-park that desire became an almost paranoiac need. She had to get away. The urgency was almost unbearable. She opened the car door and got out. Daryl brought her bag round and stood in front of her.

'Shall I take it to your room?' he asked hopefully.

'No. I hate goodbyes. Go now, drive carefully and, please, don't let me have to write that book for a long time.' Sandy kissed him firmly on the mouth, not touching him anywhere else, a dismissing kiss. Scooping up her bag, she turned and walked into the hotel without looking back. In the corridor she started to run. She had to get to her room, along the dark blue corridor, grab the keys, up the stairs, along another corridor, then into the room. She locked the door behind her. Then for a moment she stood there, irresolute, before crossing to the window. The car was gone.

She felt an extraordinary sense of relief. She was free. Free to come and go and please herself again. Just going to the loo was a pleasure. She would go out with the boys tonight.

In the bar she met Chuck, an American journalist who had just returned from Alabama, and they talked shop for a while. With the help of the generous drinks served by Rick, the barman, elation began to flow through Sandy's veins. Rick was the perfect American barman, slight, with sallow skin and slicked black hair. He was always busy – polishing glasses, slicing fruit, stashing bottles on ice. Up and down the bar he went, never missing a thing. No scandal, row or whispered intimacy passed him by and he knew everyone's private history.

'Where's the boyfriend?'

'Gone, back to New Mexico, fucked off, thank Christ.' She turned to Chuck. 'I'm not built for affairs. Don't have the stamina any more. I've been loving 'em and leaving 'em for too long now and if anyone hangs around for more than a couple of days I get bored, dreadfully bored. I just can't bear not to be free, to be my own master. I mean, he was very nice, very considerate, but I'm too old to be owned. I can't deal with it any more.'

'He didn't seem quite your style,' commented Rick. 'Bit too much of a country hick for you ... comes from the South, don't he ?'

'Well, he was born in Orlando and raised in New Mexico. Is that the South?'

'Sounded like he came from the South to me...'

It was still early evening, but Sandy was glad to accept Chuck's invitation to dinner. He did his best to cheer her up about the list of failures on her try-out, telling her it didn't necessarily mean she wouldn't be offered a job. He tried to make her laugh with stories of the crazy wild-goose chases he had been sent on.

As they were returning to the bar after dinner Sandy caught sight of Daryl's yellow shirt through the slatted swing-doors. Oh no, she thought. Chuck was already through the doors, making for the counter. She backed away quickly. Daryl had his back to her. He hadn't seen her. She ran to her room and stood there in the dark. She didn't want to see him, her mind was made up. There was a knock on the door and her heart turned over.

'It's Chuck,' came the welcome voice.

'Thank God,' she said, opening the door. 'I just don't want to see him. I don't know why, but I don't.'

'I guessed that was it. Listen, why don't we sneak out the back and go to a club? You can't stay holed up here all evening.' When they returned Daryl's car was still in the parking lot and Sandy's panic returned. She knew he was waiting for her. Chuck, always understanding, suggested a walk along the beach. The stars were vast and brilliant in the dense black sky and the tension slipped away. At two the bar would close and she would be safe. They sneaked in the back way and Chuck saw her safely to her room. As she went to the window she saw Daryl's car pull away. He had given up.

On Thursday Sandy woke with a feeling of foreboding. They would tell her today that they didn't want her. Well, on days like this you need all the strength you can give yourself, she thought, so she dressed defiantly in her skin-tight jeans, white silk shirt and high platform shoes, completing the picture with an Australian bushwacker's hat she had found perched on a parking meter at 4.00 am in New York. Her appearance created the sensation she intended on arrival at the office and the laughter level rose high enough to cause a few executive frowns.

'Well, thank you very much,' said Mike Hoy, coming over to

Sandy's desk. 'And where were you last night? I got lumbered with your boyfriend. He was sitting waiting for you all evening. You are a shit, Sandy, why didn't you tell him you weren't turning up?'

'Oh Mike, I'm sorry. But I *had* said goodbye to him. I just didn't want to see him anymore. I told him I wanted to be alone. Chuck took me out to dinner. I saw him there but I couldn't face it.'

'Well, we felt sorry for him, sitting there. He talked to Jim and Susan and me all night. I wouldn't mind, he's a nice enough bloke, but I can't understand half of what he says.'

'No, neither can I and I've had time to get me ears tuned!' Jim came over and introduced himself. Another try-out from an evening paper in Fleet Street, he and his wife had arrived while Sandy was away.

'Sorry, Jim,' said Sandy. 'I just hadn't expected him to turn up.'

'Oh, that's OK. We found him very interesting. He talked a lot about taxes here and financial law, you know. We would like to settle here and it was useful. We took him back to our place for a drink and finished off the brandy. Can't say I feel too great this morning.' He smiled. 'We booked him into our hotel at about 3.00 am. He said he had nowhere to stay.'

'I guessed he must be nearby. I had a phone call at 8.55 am but I didn't answer it. With any luck he'll be on his way to New Mexico by now. Listen, let me buy you a drink this evening, to make up.'

Sandy was called across to her boss's desk. He was a nice man, retaining, as Scotsmen always do, his soft burr. Sandy felt that he was never quite sure about her. She knew he liked her work, but suspected that he found her independence abrasive in a woman.

'The management would like you to remove your hat,' he started cautiously. 'They don't like it.'

'Bugger them,' she replied tactlessly. 'Nobody tells me what to wear. You employ the inside of my head not the outside. Anyway, I like it.'

'Well,' he said, trying not to laugh, 'that was the message, and are you free for lunch?' Here it comes, she thought, and she was right. They didn't want her.

Of course, by the time she returned, the whole office knew and she received a few commiserations. There was a message waiting for her at the desk. One for her and one for Mike Hoy. Scrawled on the pink paper was the time the message was received, 1.20 pm and 'Please ring Detective Sergeant Gabbard at West Palm Beach police station.' She called to Mike. They looked at each other in astonishment. What could they have done?

'Are you sure there wasn't any message with it,' she asked the desk clerk, 'anything to say what it was about?'

'I don't know... er... yeah, I think he mentioned something to do with some guy called Daryl.' Daryl! What could he have done? The memory of the tapes tumbled in her brain; had he committed suicide, crashed, was this the headline he was after?

'Oh Mike, you ring. Go on, be a love, I'm scared.'

'Oh no. He was your bleeding boyfriend.'

'I'm not going to... I'm going to pretend I didn't get it.'

'You have to, Sandy, they know you're here. Go on, I'll dial.'

The voice on the other end connected her quickly and she was immediately asked whether she knew Daryl Golden.

'Yes I do, has something happened to him?'

'We'd like you to come to the station straightaway. Please, miss, it's not something we can discuss on the phone.'

'Can't I come later? I'm working.'

'Either you come straight away or we will come and fetch you.' The voice on the other end had become menacing.

'Oh my God,' said Sandy to Mike, 'I have to go there. They won't tell me what has happened. I don't know if he's dead or what.'

Nervous, her face loose in a half-hysterical smile, Sandy went through the door.

The story of Daryl Golden was over.

PART TWO
PAUL JOHN KNOWLES

9:
14 November
West Palm Beach,
Florida

9:
14 November,
West Palm Beach,
Florida

THERE IS NOTHING COSY ABOUT WEST PALM BEACH POLICE STATION. The authentic sights and scents of the institution are all there: hard, glossy walls and floors redolent of disinfectant, well-worn oak desks and chairs, a few framed testimonials on the walls. The policemen, too, look the same as they do all over the world: alert, suspicious, the possessors of an instant and eternal curiosity.

Sergeant Gabbard was no exception. A shortish, stocky man with curling iron-grey hair and piercing blue eyes, he looked up from his cluttered desk as I stood on the threshold of his office, then he rose, picking up a report from the top of the pile.

'I'm Sandy Fawkes, you asked me to come in... about Daryl Golden. What's the matter, has he had an accident or something ?'

'Sit down, Miss Fawkes. Tell me, what is your relationship with this... er... Daryl Golden?'

'Well, he's a friend. A man I met a week ago who drove me here from Atlanta. He should be on his way to New Mexico. Why, what's happened to him?'

Gabbard looked grave. I was half-aware of policemen in shirtsleeves passing the desk with curious glances in my direction. My mind was racing but nothing prepared me for the reply.

'Do you know a Mrs Susan MacKenzie?'

'No. Oh, er, yes,' I stammered, remembering Jim's wife whom I had met briefly.

'Your friend attempted to rape her this morning.'

I looked at him in total disbelief. Then my wounded pride reacted.

'Good God... and he wasn't even a good poke!'

And with that cheap, flippant and defensive remark I sealed my fate for what was to become a nightmare two weeks. Sergeant Gabbard's face was interesting to watch as the outraged male in him fought first shock then laughter, a most unsuitable reaction in view of the seriousness of the charge. I apologised quickly, knowing I had made a tactical blunder.

'Tell me about it,' I said, 'When did it happen? I just don't understand.' Surely this couldn't be the great event that was going to make headlines?

'Mrs MacKenzie says that he was driving her to the hairdresser's this morning when he pulled the car off the road and asked her to make love to him. When she refused he pulled a gun on her.'

'A gun? I didn't know he had a gun.'

'She thinks it was a pistol. She struggled to get out of the car and he grabbed her by the hair but somehow she got the door open and ran screaming into the road and he drove off. She managed to stop a passing car and they took her to a phone and called the police. One of our squad cars spotted the car heading out of West Palm Beach and flagged it down. Before the officer had a chance to get out of the car the man levelled a sawn-off shotgun out of the window and said "Hold it right there." The police officer just fell right out of his car, onto the ground, but no shots were fired.'

I sat there, absolutely dumbfounded. I couldn't believe what was happening. I had never seen a gun, let alone two. Where had he kept them? And oh, those jokes! My skin was hot with embarrassment. Sergeant Gabbard looked straight at me.

'So perhaps, Miss Fawkes, you had better tell us all you know about this man.'

'Quite frankly there isn't much to tell. I met him in a bar in Atlanta and he offered to drive me here as he was on his way to see his lawyer in Miami. No, I don't know the lawyer's name, but he didn't see him. His father owns a small chain of restaurants in New Mexico. He's the business manager.' I was thinking aloud, meandering: 'Of course there is the business of the tapes, maybe he was right after all.' Sergeant Gabbard looked up quickly from the notes he was writing.

'What tapes?'

Trying desperately to sort out thoughts, facts and emotions, I told him of the mysterious tapes that held the secret of Daryl's past. At that moment, I think neither of us believed in their existence but it was an odd, intriguing aspect to an event which seemed entirely out of character with the man I knew. While my statement was being typed out, I swivelled in my chair to look at the room which suddenly seemed to have been filled with the slightly hysterical sound of my voice. There, sitting behind me, were Susan and her husband Jim, the expression on her face reflecting mine – self-conscious, the slightly nervous tick of a smile, a kind of guilty self-importance and, in her case, physical shock.

I walked over to her to apologise, though I wasn't sure quite what for and all the while I fought resentment; so he too had preferred blondes. Much later I was to appreciate what a marvellous display of instinctive courage she had performed; that fear of the gun which is ingrained in the average American was unknown to Susan and she had fought back, not acquiesced, as so many would have done.

Susan had been helping the identification expert while I was being questioned and we found an image that vaguely resembled Daryl. Crossing the room to a computer screen, Sergeant Gabbard called up a file and I leaned over to examine it. On it were two photographs, one full-face, one profile. The pictures had a handsome, youthful intensity. And they were him. Beneath them was a six-figure number and a name. Paul John Knowles. I had been travelling for a week with a common criminal. Daryl Golden had never existed. I felt sick with shame, and betrayed. Handing them back I found the sergeant examining my face intently.

'That's him. Only he hasn't got the moustache now, I made him shave it off.' I had spoken automatically and it was only as I saw the twinkle return to Gabbard's eyes that I realised the profound absurdity of the situation. There I was with a known criminal and rapist, bossy to the last. Trying not to laugh out loud, I asked who Knowles was and what he had done.

'He's an ex-parolee. He jumped his parole in Jacksonville earlier this year.'

'Oh no. My God, no wonder he knew so much about it when I went to interview William Saxbe! He drove me to the place.' Neither of us could resist the laughter now, the irony was too much for both of us. And Daryl must have laughed too as he had sat outside in his car while his companion chatted to the Attorney-General. He had made a fool out of me, but it was too rich for rancour.

'Well, what's next?'

'I don't think we'll need you anymore, Miss Fawkes. We have the number of his car and we'll put an alert out. We'll try and get hold of this lawyer in Miami. He hasn't any record for violence so I think those tapes were just eyewash but we'll look into it just the same. Thank you for your help.' Sergeant Gabbard returned to the hotel with us to check my passport and on the way he pointed out the place where the attack had taken place. A semi-circle of open space flanked by spindly trees; it didn't look very sinister, except for the policemen searching the ground for clues and Susan's purse which she had lost during her flight.

After Gabbard had gone I headed straight for the bar. Mike Hoy was there, agog for the details. Jim and Susan had hoped to keep quiet about the incident, but already several people were in possession of half the facts and Rick was busier than ever, polishing glasses, piecing the whispers together.

Journalists, like young doctors, hide their feelings with a humour that can seem hard and callous to outsiders. The jokes that night weren't kind. Fawkes outstripping a rapist was a key theme, but Susan suffered the fate of all rape victims. Doubt and distrust of her virtue. The collective male ego present was convinced she had led him on, her husband's kindness was restructured as weakness, her prettiness was her fault. It was the typical cruelty of dissatisfied talents. Susan and Jim felt it and left early.

Alone in the crowd, still wearing the absurd bushwacker's hat and grateful for the endless supply of numbing drinks, I wondered where Daryl was now. Did he feel hunted? He must have known that I knew by now; was he thinking of me? This time last night he had been standing at this exact spot at the bar. I wanted to turn the clock back, tell him anything, that I would stay, love him, anything to prevent what was happening to him. Poor man, fighting to stay free, while all these people stood cheerfully in the bar. No wonder he had felt uncomfortable in the Fontainbleu, had enjoyed being here so much.

Nobody noticed when I was called to the desk around 9.00 pm. Two large men stood there; there was no need to ask where they came from.

'You Sandy Fawkes?'

'Yes.'

'You're coming with us.'

I had no chance to call to my friends for protection. My arms were pinned firmly against my sides and I was led to the waiting squad car. The silence was menacing. No, they couldn't tell what it was about, they had instructions to take me in, that was all. At the station the atmosphere had changed from amiable courtesy to outright hostility. For some reason I was on the wrong side of the law. I was put into a small room with pale green walls and no window. It was about eight-foot square. When I turned round the two men were blocking the open door.

'What's going on?' I asked belligerently, unaware that my appearance would probably lead any policeman anywhere to consider me part of the Symbionese Liberation Army. They didn't reply.

Three men came into the tiny room. I had seen two of them on my first visit, they had smiled easily in the crowded office. They weren't smiling now as they took the seats behind the desk. The other, a short swarthy man, sat to one side. Again I asked what the hell was going on.

The swarthy man placed a well-thumbed card before me, then intoned its contents – my rights. Looking from one grim face to another, I felt panic. Somehow I had to protect myself, no one else would. Reaching into my handbag I fumbled for a notebook and pen.

'Listen, I know nothing of your law or what this is about, I intend to write all this down.'

My notebook was snatched from my hand, the bag hurled into the corner. Livid with rage I got up to retrieve them and was flung against the wall. The swarthy man snarled. 'We're not interested in your rights, lady. This is a criminal case now and you are going to stay here till you have answered our questions. Got it?'

Anger and alcohol sent my blood racing. How dare they treat a British citizen like this?

'What about the one phone call I can make? I want to make it now.'

'You'll make it when it suits us, not before.'

I looked at the two younger men sitting impassively behind the desk. No hope of appeal there; pointless, too, to head for the door. They were all armed. I was beginning to shake.

'Take her purse and have it examined.' One of the younger men left the room with the bag and I did a swift mental survey of what was in it. No Tampax, at least, I thought with absurd relief. And then a saving, humorous memory came to my rescue. When my friend Henrietta had been arrested for chucking a brick through the window of South Africa House after Sharpeville, she too had been told to empty her handbag. As she had tipped out the contents her diaphragm rolled out, wobbling a lunatic course along the entire length of the bench. Just hang on, Fawkes, I told myself, they can't do anything to you. Soon it will be just another adventure to tell the boys. Relax.

'Alright,' I said, 'but let me tell you one thing first. I'm a journalist and even if I can't write things down I have total recall and anything you do to me will be reported. I am perfectly willing to co-operate with you as I did this afternoon, but don't think you can bully me because I won't put up with it. Now what do you mean by a criminal case?'

Booze and bravery.

'Knowles, the man you identified this afternoon,' said the swarthy one, his face still dark with anger, 'has attacked a woman in a wheelchair, a paraplegic, and has abducted her sister. The woman is still missing.' He paused, his eyes implacable, hard. He had me cornered at last, and was evidently enjoying it. 'A woman is missing, got it? We also have reason to believe that Knowles may have been involved in the murder of two people in Milledgeville recently.'

'Murder? Murder? He couldn't have done... how could he when he has been with me all week?' Ever the champion of the underdog, I was defending him instinctively.

'The important thing at this moment is the woman, we have to find her. We want you to try and remember everything about him, any places he may have mentioned, any friends or names.' I looked at him blankly, there was so much, so little. Oh God, it was this time last week. Last Thursday. All that laughter and dancing. How little attention I had paid to that soft voice droning on, all I could remember was the girlfriend in Macon and the lawyer in Miami.

'I just can't think.' My hand squeezed the bridge of my nose, as I tried to concentrate. 'There was a case in Atlanta he was settling, a girl in San Francisco, I think he said she was English... he had been to every state in the Union.'

He sat there staring at me, his relentless gaze making no secret of his intuitive dislike for me. I was not one of the respectable breed of women content to keep home for some man, but an adventuress, a woman who had said a man was not a good poke.

'The Georgia authorities say the murders were so violent they think they must have been done by two people. Where were you on November 5 and 6?' My intestines were in turmoil, my heart swooped, plummeted, my whole body took the blow. They were going to accuse me of murder. A confusion of images, films, headlines dashed through my brain. Outwardly I was rescued again by rage, panic and pride. How dare they suggest I could be involved in anything as sordid as murder? I turned to the two silent witnesses, rigid with self-control.

'On the 5th I was in New York chasing after a celebrity, on the 6th I was in Washington chasing after a former Vice President. You can check by my hotel bills which are in my handbag, and I want to tell you right now that I will not take this sort of treatment, I will not be bullied by accusations like that. This is a disgraceful way to treat someone that you want to help you. You can ask me any questions you like but I will not talk to that man.'

'That man' rose to the bait beautifully, spitting out: 'If you don't co-operate I can have you put in the slammer!'

'You can do what you fucking like,' came my courteous reply.

The following day I was to pass the row of cells on my way to be fingerprinted and mentally I crossed myself, thankful for the ignorance of my courage. Those medieval structures with a nine-inch barred square in the door might have honeyed even my waspish tongue. With his head ducked to disguise a tiny glimmer of amusement, one of the young men hurriedly left the room, returning after a brief absence with news of a phone call for my angry antagonist. I knew then I had won, he would not be returning.

'Thank Christ he's gone,' I sighed, turning in a comradely manner to the two inquisitors who remained. I smiled to show that I had every intention of being helpful.

'He gets like that sometimes,' said one of them, 'doesn't mean anything, but he's really worried about this case.' And with that we settled down to the long night's work. We were soon on first-name terms and, as the shock subsided, my skilled journalist's memory began to reconstruct the week. The torn front page of the *Constitution*, the sleep as we passed Macon, the lack of cash, where we stayed, his knowledge of the roads, no detail was too trivial, each day was analysed minutely for clues. Hour after hour the interrogation went on. Occasionally there was the welcome interruption of a new report. The whole station was at work. There was still no news of Mrs Barbara Tucker, the abducted woman, and the beige Volkswagen they were travelling in. More memories. Daryl – I was still unable to make the transition to reality – had pointed out the number of these cars on the road, telling me that they were now one of the largest sellers in the States. Safety in numbers, for him if not for her.

First came the information that I had been cleared of being in the Milledgeville area on the night of 5 November. My panic began to subside. I still could not believe that my golden-haired companion was capable of murder; surely he would be able to clear himself too...? And yet he *had* mentioned being in the Macon area several times. Then came the news that the Chevrolet had been found abandoned in a street near Barbara Tucker's house, the elegant clothes still hanging on the back rail. On the front seat was the mottled leather briefcase with the torn front page of the *Atlanta Constitution* inside.

'That more or less confirms it,' said my interrogator. 'Only a criminal with a personal interest in the case would act like that, it's a sort of reminder of his deeds. The number plates of the car have been changed too. Our detectives are checking the registration number of the engine right now.' Minutes later another detective came in.

'We found it. The Last Will and Testament of Paul John Knowles, leaving his entire estate to his lawyer and his parents. Got the name of the lawyer and his address. Yep, in Miami.' So the tapes were true. That tingle at the back of my neck as we sat high above Atlanta last Friday was justified. Through my concern for Mrs Tucker, my wounded pride, my horror at the Milledgeville murders, I could feel a healthy professional interest beginning to grow. This could indeed be a big story.

It was a long wait while the car was being checked. The two men left the room, shutting the door behind them. The small windowless room with the barred exit and no human company to divert my raging thoughts was stifling, claustrophobic. I knew it was deliberate, leaving me there to stew in my own bitter anxiety. I couldn't stand it. I went to the door and tried the handle. Miraculously it opened, but two men advanced quickly to shut it again.

'I can't stay in this room with the door shut, I'll go mad,' I pleaded, deleting the word 'claustrophobic' from my mind, they wouldn't understand it. 'Look, I'm obviously not going to run anywhere. For God's sake don't shut me in there alone.' They shut the door. I opened it again.

'I'll stand here by the door and you can keep an eye on me,' I said firmly. Perhaps it was my British arrogance, perhaps they knew they had no right to shut me away, anyway they conceded. I stood in the open doorway and watched the activities in the main office, able to overhear telephone calls repeating that there was still no sign of the Volkswagen and its occupants.

Later my interviewers returned, with a friendly cup of coffee for me and news of the Chevrolet Impala, my Snoopy dream car that I had driven along the highway with such pleasure and pride. It was a brand new model and had belonged to William Bates, a 32-year-old man from Lima, Ohio. His car, papers and credit cards were missing too. The hotels at which we stayed confirmed that Mr and Mrs William Bates had registered there on the nights of 8 and 9 November. I had been living on a dead man's credit cards.

It was 3.00 am before I was let out of the interrogation room. I knew by then that two men from the Georgia Bureau of Investigation were driving through the night, taking the same road I had driven with Knowles. I was to report at the station at 10.30 a.m. for more questioning. Another detective from Brewton, Alabama, was heading my way too. The trail of credit cards was being traced across the States. Knowles's boast that he had visited them all could be confirmed at gas stations, motels, shops. Files on unsolved crimes were being reopened all over America.

Sipping a coffee in the main room while my statement was being typed out, I tried to diagnose my feelings. My brain was opening and shutting doors at a speed faster than light, sifting, shifting, organising its defences. The atmosphere in the station was friendlier now and I received several congratulations on my narrow escape but I was unable to feel a personal sense of danger. The man I had known, who had run to the pharmacist to get balm for my burn, who had guarded my money against thieves, opened doors, driven me safely along miles of deserted roads, laughed at my jokes, listened to my childhood stories, had never been a threat to me, of that I was sure. The sickening fact that he had killed at all, was perhaps killing Mrs Tucker at that very moment, was disorientating enough; I had no energy to spare for self-indulgent speculation.

At 3.45 am, I was allowed my legal phone call. Big deal American justice. There was no offer to escort me home by squad car, so I rang Mike Hoy.

'Jesus Christ, Sandy, I had no idea! I thought you had sloped off to bed early. Somebody said they thought you'd gone off with the police but we were all too drunk to check.' Thank you, friends.

At 4.15 am, I stepped out of the station into the warm damp air, seven hours of tiered horror behind me, layer on layer of evidence and emotion.

'Oh Mike, he's a murderer, isn't it awful, and he's kidnapped a local woman and the car was stolen and the owner has been missing for four months, it's all so dreadful, and I travelled with him and he might have killed any of us, what have I done?' My voice was rising fast.

'Stop that, Fawkes,' he said sharply. 'You can tell me about it tomorrow. Listen, I've only just got to bed and I've got to be up in four hours.' He was right, this was no time to let go, there was too much to do. Mike and I shared the same boss, he would have to be informed.

'Jesus Christ,' said Mike, 'he'll shit a brick,' and with that cheering thought he parked the car and deposited me at my door with instructions to get some sleep.

I flung the offending hat into the corner of the room. I never wanted to see it again. I had been up for 20 hours but I knew I wouldn't be able to sleep immediately. I wondered whether Knowles was out there somewhere needing help. What was going on in that strange mind? Lying back on the pillow at last, I felt my eyes would never close again. Exactly a week ago I had been in his arms. How could I have made such a mistake? Then, like hot metal flooding my veins, came the memory of that first morning, the sense of evil in the room that had thrust me headlong to the door. Good God, I *had* known. Then, as silent tears rolled down my cheeks, I fell asleep.

In the morning, I called my daughter Kate in London to tell her it looked as if my return would be delayed a few days. I told her briefly about the trouble I was in.

'Oh, Mum, are you alright, you might have been killed.' Her light and tremulous voice came across the miles. It was wonderful to be called Mum again. I longed for home, my children and the joyous welcome our dog, Muldoon, would have for me.

'Listen, darling, I know it's hard but don't tell anyone yet, the *Express* don't know what I've been up to in the States and I'd like to keep it quiet for a while. I'll ring the New York office on Sunday, so keep in touch with the foreign desk. I've spoken to Jo and she's fine. I'll be back as soon as I can, I promise.'

It was a cruel and thoughtless thing to have done, telling an 18-year-old girl that her mother had been in danger for her life and asking her to keep the news to herself, but my sensibilities were limited to myself. Poor Kate suffered in silence loyally.

10: 15 November West Palm Beach, Florida

WEST PALM BEACH POLICE STATION WAS STILL BUSY WHEN I ARRIVED. Mrs Tucker had not been found, nor had the Volkswagen. I was introduced to Georgia Bureau of Investigation (GBI) agents Gerald Coffee and Charles Osborne, two big, burly men who looked as if they ate bricks for breakfast. Their faces wore that look of shrewd friendliness that made all policemen appear alike to me. We were all a little bleary-eyed; I had had only four-and-a-half hours sleep and they had driven through the night. I began again the account of that fateful week, the meeting in Atlanta, the existence of the tapes, the long drive. This time I was being taped; a small irony.

'Do you think he was a homosexual?' they asked.

'No, I don't think so. Quite frankly I asked him once, so many of my friends are it didn't seem important and since he couldn't make it in bed...' It was difficult to know what these big hunks of manhood were thinking, but I was too tired to be anything but direct.

'...but he managed it a couple of times, enough to make me think he was inexperienced rather than gay.' Candour of that kind they were certainly not expecting and I tried to soften it with a smile. 'Tell me about the case,' I said. 'I really know very little. Yesterday was so confusing. There was so much going on I didn't take in the details.' Cunning little cow, I thought, you just want to have all the facts first-hand.

'We are investigating the murder of two people. A Mr Carswell Carr and his 15-year-old daughter, Mandy. The reason we asked whether he was homosexual was that he met Mr Carr in a gay bar, one that they all go to.' Gays in Georgia? The mind boggled a bit. 'And the killing was kinda sadistic.'

I couldn't remember a child being mentioned the night before. I felt a sick flow of shame washing away my momentary self-confidence. I braced every nerve; their faces seemed to hold the story, the picture, of all they had seen.

'We still don't know if Mr Carr died of his wounds or of a heart attack from the assault, but he had been tormented. He was stabbed with a pair of scissors, but the wounds were just jabs. Twenty-seven of them. Mr Carr had his hands tied behind his back and it kinda looked as if the attacker had enjoyed himself.' There was nothing to say. We looked at each other in silence. On their faces, as there must have been on mine, were pity, horror and that terrible excitement that proximity to violent death always brings.

Gerald Coffee's voice rose a little. 'The room looked as if it had been attacked by an animal. The mirrors were smashed, the furniture upturned and slashed, books thrown everywhere. It looked like someone wanted to make it look like a robbery... at first we thought it must be the work of two people.' He looked at me slyly. Was this another trap? Or had he heard already of my trigger-happy temper?

'When exactly did this happen?' I asked calmly.

'We don't know the exact time – nobody saw Mr Carr leave the bar – but it was either on the night of the 5th or early on the 6th.'

Oh God, two nights before I met him. The night I had been cavorting around Washington with Laurie Bryant. Guy Fawkes night in Britain, when effigies are burnt and fireworks lit to commemorate the man who tried to blow up the Houses of Parliament in the 17th century. I didn't want to ask the next question.

'And the child?'

'She was strangled and raped. We found her face down on her bed with her hands bound behind her back. At least it was attempted rape, there was no evidence of semen present.' But of course. He couldn't come.

'Listen, I'll do everything I can to help you but I must just walk around a bit. I can't take it all at once. You really believe Daryl, sorry, Knowles did it? God, that poor women, Barbara Tucker, she just doesn't stand a chance.' They gave me a coffee to calm me down. It was tasteless but very welcome.

'We'd like you to look at some pictures, Sandy; a lot of things were taken from the house. Mrs Carr gave us a list but obviously she wasn't in a state to think too clearly. Maybe you can identify some of them.'

In his hand was a pack of photographs. They looked like the homely snapshots that Americans throughout the world present to strangers. The first one, a portrait of Mr Carr smiling behind horn-rimmed glasses, meant nothing. The next one did though.

Mr Carswell Carr smiling again, glass in hand, among a group of friends. He was wearing a smart, bright yellow, double-breasted blazer. The one Daryl had worn in the Polaris lounge at the top of the Hyatt Regency in Atlanta when he told me of the tapes which contained the dark secret of his past.

So it was true. He was a killer.

The officers' excitement at the first real identification was infectious; this was no time to brood. They wanted a list of all the clothes and possessions I had seen. Trained as a fashion artist in the days when the French Haute Couture guarded their secrets ferociously, I could remember everything.

I described the brocade dinner jackets with matching shirts and pants. They produced the pictures. The patent shoes he had polished so lovingly with the buckles that had gleamed on the dance-floor. Yes, they had the pictures. The mottled brown leather briefcase that augmented his businessman's image, the matching shaving case he had used to shave off his moustache for my delight. The white belt that had fitted my waist and his slender hips, even the half-bottle of bourbon we had taken to my room that first night – oh no, don't tell them what you used it for, Fawkes – every single garment I had so admired on my handsome escort had belonged to the dead man.

As they shuffled through the pile of pictures they paused for a moment, unsure whether to show me the next.

'These are the pictures of the place as we found it,' said Coffee. 'You don't have to look if you don't want to.' But I did. I needed to. Needed to see the reality of the man I had known, I needed to be rescued by hate.

There were photographs of the corpses and the house in chaos. Carswell Carr naked, face down on the bed, hands bound behind his back, his body covered with small inch-long wounds. And Mandy, also naked and bound, face up, her eyes closed forever, a cloth round her neck. Her mouth was a dark cavity.

'He had pushed her pantyhose so far down her throat it took the doctor fifteen minutes to get it out. Her mother is a nurse, she was working that night. She found them when she came home in the morning.'

That poor woman. To live forever with that knowledge, that sight, to lose a daughter of 15; I knew the tears, could imagine the pain. It put my ordeal in perspective. I was not grieving for a lost child, I was merely having a tough time. There was a lot to do. We went through the list of missing property once again. No I hadn't seen a dark green hold-all, he hung his clothes on a rack. Yes, I knew the clock, the electric digital clock-radio with the torn wires.

'Did you see what time it had stopped, we could place the time of the killings if you can remember that.'

'No, I saw the digits flicking past, but I'm sure I didn't see it set.' I played the scene over and over again in my mind, him sitting on the edge of the bed, that small knowing grin on his face, but there was nothing there. I told them the white belt was still in my possession back at the hotel; they wanted permission to search my room. Was I still under suspicion? No, but there might be something I had forgotten. The thought of strangers going through your underwear in your absence is never very pleasant, but I had no choice.

While they were away, I was fingerprinted to eliminate my prints from the car. While I waited for them to return I tried to find out more about Knowles's background. Who was this man who had taken me in so completely, who had killed others but spared me?

Paul John Knowles was not 33 years old but 28, born in Orlando, Florida, as he had said. His family he had described accurately too; a father, mother and two older brothers and sisters, but they were not the middle-class owners of a small chain of restaurants. His father was a carpenter. His parents lived in a modest area in the back streets of Jacksonville, Florida. It was here he had been raised and here that he had had his first brushes with the law, nothing spectacular: petty burglaries, joy-rides in stolen cars, other minor offences. He always got caught, he had even been sentenced for breaking and not entering. In the previous ten years he had been in and out of reformatories, correctional institutions and prisons, spending an average of seven months of each year of adulthood inside. He had been paroled that May, but was in trouble again by July. This time he had jumped, and had been on the move ever since.

I was also able to catch up on the details of the Tucker case. Having abandoned the Chevrolet after trying to rape Susan MacKenzie, Knowles had made his way to Locust Street where, selecting a house at random, he had knocked on the back door of No 705. When the door was opened by Beverly Mabee, Barbara Tucker's twin sister, he told her he was Bob Williams from the Internal Revenue Service. Miss Mabee, 31, is a victim of cerebral palsy and she was confined to a wheelchair.

Once inside, Knowles dropped the pretence. He told Miss Mabee that he needed a car and a hostage because the police were after him for a robbery. They sat and waited for Barbara Tucker to return from her job at the local radio station, WJNO. When she returned with her six-year-old son, Dale, Beverly Mabee was already tied to her bed. Knowles tied up Dale and forced Mrs Tucker into her car, the beige Volkswagen. They drove off at about 7.00 pm on Thursday evening. Beverly Mabee had eventually freed herself and called the police. The search was on.

Charles Osborne and Gerald Coffee returned, flinging the watch I had bought Kate in Miami on the desk.

'You've spoilt it,' I cried. 'You've made a scratch right across its face.'

'We think this is Mandy's missing watch. It fits the description. She wore one with a clear face through which you could see the works.'

'No, it's not,' I protested. 'I bought this watch myself.'

I was nursing my daughter's present, trying to remove the marks with my thumb, when I suddenly remembered.

'The fashion watch! He gave me a kid's fashion watch, I'd forgotten all about it. I hated it, that's why I didn't wear it. I put it with the souvenirs from Cape Kennedy. Listen, I've got the receipt for this one in my bag.' But as I fumbled in the jumble, grateful for the second day running that I am not the sort who throws away receipts, they were out of the door on their way to my hotel. They were back in no time carrying the childish object I had thought was so unseemly in Miami. It matched the pictures. Mandy had worn the watch face down; some local fad no doubt.

At lunchtime, there was still no news of Barbara Tucker or Knowles. There was little more for me to do except wait at the hotel. But then, walking out, I had a sudden thought.

'What if he comes after me? He knows my room number and it's right by the back exit. And I'm the only one who can identify him, connect him directly with all this.'
I think I scared them almost as much as I did myself. Suddenly, I was back in the squad car again and this time the huge bulk of the officer beside me was comforting. Within minutes of our arrival the manager and porters had been summoned to change my room to one without an accessible balcony. My telephone extension was kept the same, just in case he rang.

'I expect he is far away by now, but you'll feel better,' said the officer as he left. For the first time in a long while I felt sorry to see the back of a policeman. At 6.00 pm, the pictures of Knowles and the missing woman flashed across the television screen along with the information that he was armed and dangerous.

Friday night found me, inevitably, at the bar. I needed the company. By now everyone knew the story and all were eager for information. For once I was thankful for their blanket of unfeeling humour. For a while, till they tired of the subject and turned to the more gratifying one of their own grievances, I was the centre of attention, always one of my favourite positions. My ex-boss came in, partly to say good-bye, partly to see if I was alright, but mostly to check out what I had said to the police about my position on the paper. I assured him I had covered their interests by saying that I was freelancing for my holiday and he went away satisfied. Around 8.00 pm, I told the desk clerk I was nipping out to the nearest hamburger joint and that if the police wanted me to send somebody to fetch me. I was away for barely 15 minutes.

'There was a call for you while you were away... I think it was that man who was with you earlier this week. He had a very deep voice.' I couldn't believe it. Obviously there was no message. I found that now I knew, I was desperate to talk to him. I had to try to fuse the man I knew with the other, the murderer. Most of all I longed to ask why, why didn't you kill *me*?

I stayed in my room by the phone but there were no more calls from him, only minor queries from the police. The call that I had had seemed to set the seal on Mrs Tucker's fate. He must be on the run again.

On Saturday at 11.00 am, I had an appointment with a Sergeant Brewer of the State of Alabama in connection with the murder of Ben Sherrod, the president of City Utilities Construction Company of Miami. When I arrived the station was electric with action.

'We've found Mrs Tucker,' someone flung at me. 'She's alive. He left her tied up in a motel and she freed herself this morning.' I was smiling my relief when the bad news came. 'He has kidnapped one of our men and is heading north.' Orders were bouncing off the walls as police for miles around were mobilised. The phones rang incessantly as off-duty troopers volunteered to help in the search.

'How did Barbara Tucker survive?' I asked when one of them had time to spare.

'Guts. Sheer guts. She just kept calm and cool and kept him talking and just went along with him. She is very lucky and very, very brave. She was a redhead too,' he said, laughing.

'Well, well. Where were they?' Answering this one didn't give him much pleasure.

'At Fort Pierce. They checked into the Skyway Motel at 10.30 pm on Thursday night and stayed there all day yesterday. When the pictures were flashed on the TV he tied her up in their room and got away. She managed to free herself early this morning.' Fort Pierce was barely 40 miles away, right on Route US 1. The Volkswagen must have been in the parking lot all that time. Osborne and Coffee had driven right past it on their way south; no wonder they weren't pleased. Now they had lost him again.

The policemen who weren't answering calls were standing around in worried groups. The Volkswagen had been found in Perry, near the northern border of Florida, indicating that

Knowles had driven through the night, using his familiarity with the back routes to escape. The missing man was State Trooper Charles E Campbell.

'He must have stopped Knowles for questioning,' one of them explained to me. 'He must've got out of the car. I can't understand it, Charlie's a good cop. He didn't even call the station first. The terrible thing is, his best friend was killed this time last year. He was a trooper too. We've got to find him.' Knowles had apparently abducted a State Trooper, fully armed, in his own squad car. The interview with Sergeant J Marlon Brewer from the State of Alabama took less than an hour. He was investigating the murder of Ben Sherrod, the president of a Miami company. Sherrod had been found bound and shot in Brewton, Alabama, on 21 October, but apart from telling him that Knowles had mentioned Alabama I was unable to be of help. I promised to keep in touch with the station and to let them know my movements, but my importance to them was over. There was an almighty air and road alert being mounted.

In the middle of the afternoon the phone rang, it was Sergeant Gabbard again. 'Sandy, he's heading south again. They found the patrol car abandoned and it looks like he might try and get back to you. He's still got the trooper and we think he's got somebody else as well, another hostage. We're putting a squad car guard on the hotel. If he gets in touch with you, agree to anything he says. If he tries to arrange a meeting or something, call us straight away. You'll be alright, we'll protect you.' My knees were shaking like a suspension bridge in a hurricane. Fucking hell, I had landed right in the middle of a B-film scenario. Shoot-out at the OK corral. I could see it all: the wooded copse where we would meet, the burst of floodlight, me flinging myself to the ground as the thunder of gunfire leapt across my prostrate body, his body gushing blood, my kneeling crying beside it. Then a chill, extremely practical thought nudged its way into the drama. If one of their own coppers, fully armed, had got himself into the position where he was kidnapped in his own patrol car, could I rely on the rest of them to be smart enough to miss me? And mulling over the fact that they hadn't been able to find him when he was only 40 miles from their own door and that I wasn't sure that they were entirely convinced of my innocence, I didn't feel exactly over-confident of my chances in a confrontation. I stood by the window quietly praying that he wouldn't ring. As I looked out the first patrol car swept into the car park.

I definitely needed a drink. There aren't many occasions when I don't. I headed downstairs to the bar. I told both the manager and the desk clerk that if any calls came they must get hold of me immediately and explained why the hotel was being circled by squad cars. The situation was scary and desperately exciting and everybody enjoyed being in on the act. Each time the door opened all heads swivelled and when I returned to my room, carrying a scotch to augment the two large ones I had gulped down in rapid succession, a couple of the reporters escorted me along the corridor. I stayed there watching the squad cars pass back and forth and every now and again one of the lads from the bar would check to see if I was OK. The police rang a couple of times to find out if I had heard anything. They had lost all trace of Knowles again. There was no news of the trooper or the other hostage, who had been identified as James E Meyer, a businessman from Delaware on a fishing holiday.

At 10.00 pm I could stand the darkened room no longer. I hadn't dared to switch on the light in case he was out there, watching. I couldn't close the curtains as I was checking the patrol every 20 minutes. I called the bar to ask someone, anyone, to fetch me. My dread that Knowles might be lurking in the corridor was now so strong that I was shaking from head to foot. The strain was too much to bear alone. After 20 minutes in the bar I went out to the desk to double-check. There was a new man on duty.

'Yes, Miss Fawkes, there was a call for you about ten minutes ago. He didn't leave a name. I tried your room but there was no reply. I'm sorry, I didn't know you were in the bar.' It wasn't his fault but I screamed at him just the same.

'Where the hell is the manager? Don't you know what's going on? There's two men's lives at stake, and mine, *mine*! He could be coming in here at any minute with a gun. What do you think the patrol cars are for, Jesus Christ...' He looked back at me, blank, indifferent, uncaring. These journalists are all the same, he was probably thinking, drink too much, get abusive, bloody nuisance. The vigil went on all night. I rang the police to explain about the phone call but there was no way of tracing it. They still had no news, no clues. I slept fully clothed, waking at every footstep outside, watching the squad cars' headlights sweep the ceiling. I thought back to last Saturday evening at

Daytona Beach. 'Yesterday, all our troubles seemed so far away.' What was it he had said...

'You won't make me regret our yesterdays will you, Sandy?' and I had held his hand in reassurance. Now I was sitting by the phone waiting for him to ring so that I could set the trap to catch him, oh Judas indeed. In the morning, I looked out at the harsh reflections on the water. The bridge was rising, steeple-shaped to allow the tall-masted deep-sea fishing yachts through. Carefree people setting out for a Sunday's enjoyment on the ocean, how I envied them their peace of mind.

It was too early to raise friends from their stupor but I could at least wait it out in the sun. Informing the desk clerk that I would be by the pool, I lay in the healing warmth, letting it sink through to my bones. I was in the pool when the phone rang. The water seemed to hold me back as I thrashed to the side and clambered out. I ran to the phone. It stopped as I lifted it. The line was dead. Not even bothering to dry myself, I raced to the desk in the hope that the clerk was trying my room. But no, he stood there placidly.

'I let it ring three times, I thought you must have gone for coffee.' Anger is useless against such blank stupidity. Yes, he agreed indifferently, it sounded like the same man, the one who had rung last night. Three times he had rung, three times I had missed it. On that brilliant Sunday morning in Florida it had an ominous biblical echo. Judas and Peter. I knew I would not hear from him again, the connection was severed.

John Harrison was manning the *Express* office in New York, always a miserable job on Sundays when the streets around the

Daily News building on 42nd Street are deserted, the noise from angry, congested cars stilled, only the view of the art deco Chrysler building, lustrous in the sky's light, enlivening the scene with its ever-changing colours. He was astounded at my news and full of gossip from London where our new editor had just arrived. I had timed my holiday deliberately to avoid those first weeks of arse-licking, but I was still anxious for news of any shifts in the hierarchy. One item gladdened my heart: the editor kept a stock of booze in his office. Any man who drank scotch in the office couldn't be all bad, I told myself. John suggested that I should write the story and phone it across later.

I thought of Knowles reading the piece of Ilie Nastase, and his shy request that I should write something like that about him. It was the least I could do for the man who had spared my life during that long journey. Already the endless scenery of the drive was beginning to haunt me. Those vigorous, succulent, bright green plants lining the road, the rich earth beneath them, the foul black swamp, all could have hidden me forever.

'He was tall, fair and handsome, with the immaculate manners of the comfortably-rich American,' I began, knowing that my readers, the ones who had written me warm and kindly letters throughout the years, would be delighted I had escaped. Thinking with some small satisfaction of the consternation the story would produce in the foreign news department as the pages appeared, I sat waiting for more news. By now the hotel was stirring and friends trooped in and out with ice-cold cans of Budweiser, the Sunday papers where Knowles was already headlines and king-sized hangovers. The patrol cars' relentless circling had upset their usual pattern of sitting round the pool and smoking pot and they were off to a more secluded spot.

I was alone in the bar watching a football game, admiring the muscular players, when the phone rang. It was Sergeant Coffee.

'We've caught him, Sandy, up in Henry County in Georgia. They found him in the woods.'

'What about the men?'

'No.' His voice was depressed. 'They weren't with him, and so far he hasn't said where they are. He may be trying to bargain for time, he might have tied them up and left them somewhere. There's a search party out but it's a pretty big area. We'll be going back in the morning, Sandy, and I want to thank you for your help.'

'Well, I'm glad it's over. I can sleep tonight. I hope you find the men. If there is anything more I can do let me know, I can always go home via Atlanta if you need me.' Relief and regret. He wasn't dead, the drama had not followed the plot, but he was behind bars now, would be forever, and I would never see him again, never get the chance to ask him why he did it, why he hadn't killed me. I rang back to see if they would give me the lawyer's name but the answer was negative, so I phoned New York with the news.

'They aren't using it, Sandy.'

'What? Why ever not, it's a bloody good story!'

'The editor says he doesn't think we want one of our ladies mixed up in something like that.'

'Ladies, my arse, what lady? They don't think of me as a lady

146

when they send me to Middle-Eastern troublespots to risk getting my legs blown off. What a load of old cobblers. I simply can't believe it. Ian McColl would have blasted it all over the front page.' Fuming and foul-mouthed with frustration, I went downstairs to watch the television news. Knowles had been spotted in Lakeland, Georgia, during lunchtime on Saturday when the blue Ford automobile had pulled into a gas station for a pack of Kool cigarettes, the two hostages in the back seat. The garage proprietor had apparently not thought it strange to see in the back of the car a uniformed policeman, who had made no sign that anything was wrong. Knowles disappeared for 24 hours until the car was seen on Highway 42 at 1.10 pm on Sunday by two Georgia sheriff's deputies. Roadblocks were set up and Knowles drove right into one, smashing his car. Firing his gun wildly he had run into the woods. It took the police less than a minute to discover that the hostages were not in the car but that Charles Campbell's empty gunbelt and hat were. The order went out. Take him alive, we must find the hostages.

For more than two hours, 200 policemen searched the woods of Henry County, using tracker dogs and helicopters. The whole neighbourhood had been alerted to keep themselves and their children behind locked doors. The hunted man came to a clearing at the edge of the woods where he was spotted by a young man in steel-rimmed spectacles and hillbilly dungarees. David Terry Clark had seen Knowles through his window, grabbed his shotgun and gone out to meet him. Knowles, who had a head injury bound with a bandana scarf, said to him simply: 'Please help me.' Clark escorted him to a nearby house where a neighbour called the police.

'Don't hurt him,' Clark told the police as Knowles was bundled away into captivity.

By 10.00 pm, I was drunk. Three days of tension had taken their toll and the roar of laughter that greeted each repetition of a current version of 'I Shot the Sheriff' found no echo in my soul. The episode had been a painful and deeply shaming experience. I was going to creep home tomorrow. My plans were changed dramatically when GBI agent Coffee rang me to ask if I would go to Macon, Georgia, the next day. Knowles was not talking. He refused to say where he had left the hostages. The two men could be anywhere out in the woods. Perhaps in view of our, er, close relationship I could get him to talk. The story was still alive.

I went upstairs and passed out for twelve hours.

11:
18 November
Macon,
Georgia

B Y THE TIME I WOKE UP, I HAD MISSED THE EARLY MORNING CONNECTION TO MACON AND HAD SEVERAL HOURS TO WAIT BEFORE THE NEXT ONE. On impulse, I rang the *Atlanta Constitution* with the story the *Daily Express* had rejected. I also promised them I would report on my interview with Knowles in his cell. It was an impulse I was to regret for two whole weeks, indeed forever.

At Atlanta airport, a vast labyrinth of endless corridors, a photographer was waiting for me with the news that a reporter would meet me at Macon. I begged him to get in touch with his office and call the reporter off. I would never get to see Knowles if the police knew my interest was professional. On the flight to Macon I read the local evening paper, the *Atlanta Journal*. The headlines were terrifying: 'Man

Captured in Hunt Suspect in 12 Slayings.' Underneath was an account of his capture and a picture of a man who bore no resemblance to the debonair dancer of last week. Unshaven and scruffy, in a dark roll-neck sweater, he looked every inch the villain. It didn't help. According to the paper, Knowles, unlike the innocent Fawkes of three days previously, had been allowed to talk to his lawyer at length. His replies to the questions at the other end of the line had been simply 'Yes' or 'No'. After that he had shut up.

Then followed a lengthy piece of conjecture based on the fact that Knowles was now known to have been in the area when each of certain murders were committed. Apart from the Carrs, William Bates and Ben Sherrod, there were two young hitch-hikers, Edward Hillard and his girlfriend, Debbie Griffin. He had been shot near Macon, her body had not been found. The paper also speculated about two unresolved slayings in Jacksonville, Knowles's home town, the murder of a band leader and his girlfriend in McDonough, Georgia, and that of a young mother from Musella, Georgia. The implication was that Knowles was responsible for all these deaths.

The flight from Atlanta to Macon took 45 minutes. We flew above the freeway we had driven along. Woods stretched to the horizon and it was easy to see the hopelessness of a search for two helpless human beings in that vastness. I wondered if Knowles would talk to me. What could I say that might persuade him not to let them die a slow and painful death out in the wilderness? How would I feel seeing him again? The contrast would be unbearable: the dancer who loved flash clothes, incarcerated, imprisoned, in uniform. Would he hate me to see him for what he really was? To see that our fantasy week had been just that? To know the carefully-foretold death had not come true? And how would I feel facing the man who had been my friend as well as my lover, knowing how he killed, knowing the trail of pain and desolation he had left behind him? When I got to Macon airport I was amazed to see Sergeant Coffee and his partner waiting to meet me.

'How on earth did you get here before me?' I asked as I walked up to them. I had seen so many policemen over the previous few days, they were all beginning to look alike. They looked at me as if I was mad. I had never seen them before. Looking back, I suppose I was slightly deranged. I was certainly emotionally exhausted and utterly confused. It didn't help that I knew I was conning them. They wanted me to get him to talk so that they could rescue their man; I wanted him to talk for a newspaper interview. Just seeing him would be a good story, a follow-up to the one that would be printed tomorrow. So I had two good reasons to be nervous.

On the steps of Bibb County jail, someone called out 'Miss Fawkes'. I ignored him but saw that the policeman who was escorting me was surprised that anyone knew of my coming here. A few steps more and I would be home and dry. Courage is one of the things you acquire early in journalism. Every day you have to face people who do not want to talk to you, whom you have to charm until they give you the story you want. When I walked through a doorway to one side of the reception area my courage was draining fast. The room was long, narrow and high, not brightly lit. Ten pairs of the hardest eyes I have ever faced turned towards me, critical, implacable. I could read their thoughts: so this is the broad who fucks killers. I could see they loathed their need of me. My small, ready-to-charm smile vanished from my face.

The introductions were perfunctory. Only one name stayed in my mind, because of its sheer incongruity. Among the mass of thick-set muscle present he stood out, not for his size – he was compact but shortish – but for his resemblance to an all-in wrestler: the close-set eyes, the shaven head, the bull neck bulging over the collar. His power was like a slap in the face. And his name was Angel, Ron Angel, GBI agent. His was the first question.

'Do you have any reason to think Knowles was a homosexual?'

'No.'

'Did you sleep with him?'

'Yes.'

If I'd been on trial and this lot had been the jury, I'd have been swinging from a lamp post in five minutes flat. They asked me if I could remember his mentioning any particular part of Georgia on our travels, whether there might be some special place where he had hidden his hostages, but I couldn't help them. We went over a few details of the Milledgeville murders and again they asked me if I had seen a dark green holdall. It was many weeks later back in London that I played back the first morning when he had collected his things from his hotel and had emerged carrying the holdall, but by then it was too late and to this day I haven't worked out where he dumped it. I was relaxing now. I seemed to have their confidence. They told me that they had already brought in Knowles's girlfriend from Macon to try to get him to talk.

'You will be going in at your own risk. We will have to lock you in with him for security reasons and he may attack you. He told his girlfriend to fuck off this morning and has refused to see her again.'

'I'll take the risk.' The woman in me had quite disappeared; the journalist, ready to do anything for a story, had taken over and I was all concentrated excitement. I picked up my bag with the notebook buried at the bottom. My knees were knocking but they were hidden by my skirt. I was wearing the same cardigan suit he had first seen me in. By then most of the men, including Ron Angel, had left the room, their business with me over. Now Angel appeared at the door, beckoning those who had remained and I was left alone. For a long time I waited, wondering if Knowles had refused to see me. It was a humiliating thought. I would just have to slope off quietly; it would be embarrassing after proclaiming our connection in print, but he had cause to hate me now. After all, I had told the police about the tapes and had identified him as the Milledgeville killer. The door opened and the two men who had driven me from the airport entered.

'We are taking you to a hotel for the night.'

'But I'm waiting to see Knowles, I thought I was going to see him.' Outside in the reception area I saw Coffee and Osborne. I tried to ask them what was happening, but I was hustled into a waiting car, the one with my luggage still in it. It was a long drive and the officers were not forthcoming with explanations about my hurried exit from Bibb County jail. From their rather grim amusement I assumed I had been right, Knowles did not want to see me. The journey had been a waste. Damn. I was hardly paying attention when they asked me if I would mind waiting a few minutes while they went into the Ambassador Hotel. They had to collect some bed linen for evidence. It was only as they stuffed the bag into the car that it dawned on me.

'Do you mean to say he was staying here? Right here in town?' He had spent Saturday night in Macon, a bare ten miles from Milledgeville, while all the police in Florida and Georgia were out hunting him. Was it cool bravura or a desperate attempt to challenge fate, to meet it head on? He had even gone into Sears on Saturday night and bought himself some clean clothes on Charles Campbell's credit card. The checkout clerk hadn't noticed, but the customer next to him had and reported it the following day. I was still sipping the first drink of the day when the reporter who had spoken to me on the steps of Bibb County jail walked in. He was lucky it wasn't my third.

'I wondered how long it would take you to find me,' I said.

'I watched which way the car went and guessed they were bringing you here.' He eased his plump and none-too-alluring body onto the stool beside me.

'I didn't get the interview, they wouldn't let me see him.'

'I know... They think you're a publicity-seeking broad out to make a name for yourself. They don't like you at all.'

'I rather gathered they didn't.'

'It's probably something to do with the fact that I told them you had already sent a story to the *Constitution* and had promised us a full account of the interview in the cell.' He grinned. You cunt, you creepy little cunt. The thought was prompt but unuttered. So it wasn't Knowles who had refused to see me, but this overfed young man with the shiny pink skin and rotund glasses who had screwed it up. My face was impassive but couldn't have been hard to read.

'Well, I had a deadline to meet,' he said half-apologetically. The following day he had four lines in the paper. I was the headline.

'You just did your paper out of one of the most interesting stories of the week. I travelled a long way for that interview.' I was in despair. I had been so close. I sensed I would never make it now; drips of poison from the local press would take care of my chances. He, in contrast, was in a chatty mood, well pleased with himself and his assignment to a major crime story.

'I was there when they brought him in. When he saw all of us waiting he threw back his head and laughed like a hyena.' The vision of his lips, full and brutal, drawn back over his teeth like a baying dog, was suddenly vivid in my mind. I knew how he must have looked. 'He was enjoying it, he loved the attention, that's why he won't tell them where the hostages are. They're all dependent on him.'

'What about the lawyer, do you know anything about him? I don't even know his name.'

'He's called Sheldon Yavitz and he's expected tomorrow. He's driving up from Miami.'

'*Driving*? Jesus, why so slow? Surely he's the one who could get him to talk?'

'Yeah, well, Knowles talked to him on Sunday night after his capture, he's the one who told him to say nothing.' And with that he slithered away. After him the reporter from the *Macon Telegraph* was welcome company and, for the first time in my life, I was in the reverse position of giving an interview, not taking it. I quite enjoyed outwitting the trap questions and in any case he was a nice bloke. Then there was a call from the local radio station. Could they drop by in the morning? I knew I was going to need all the goodwill I could get to counteract the damage already done and agreed to co-operate with everyone. I still wanted my interview.

Jess Branson of Radio WBML came round in the morning with an assistant and recording equipment. He had the easygoing look of a media person and was the first one I had met in Macon whom I felt I could talk to straight.

'Listen, love, Ron Angel told me last night that I was not to talk to anyone, not to give any publicity, and I'll tell you right now he scares the shit out of me. I can't do an interview on the radio.'

'If I square it with him and I know him, will you come on our open question show tomorrow morning at 10.30 am?' It was the golden excuse to stay. I was experienced in radio work and if he was that influential I might still get to Knowles. Yes was the answer.

'But I can't stay in this goddamn place all day.' One look at the low grassy hills and the woodlands beyond from the window had shown that I was well isolated from the action. 'After all, I am free to do what I like, I don't have to stay where they put me. Could you drop me off at the Hilton?' The three of us squeezed into the MG and on the drive to the Hilton we conspired to keep each other up to date with events. I began to feel better. The Macon Hilton probably reflects the town's importance on the map. It is all of 16 storeys high, and I carried my own bags in, but the foyer was glossy with chandeliers and bright carpeting and I felt more at home.

A hand-painted placard rested near the elevators, brown lettering on beige. 'Welcome to the Sheriffs of Georgia,' it read. I asked idly what it meant, was it anything to do with the man who had been caught yesterday? No, I was informed, it was a convention. All the 150 sheriffs from the State of Georgia were staying here. It was an annual event lasting three days; today was the first. Talk about the hornet's nest! I waited till I was safely ensconced in my room before I sat down and laughed out loud. Trust Fawkes to get herself into a situation like this. In a town where you are regarded as a murderer's moll you decide to book into a hotel that just happens to contain all the duly elected representatives of the law for miles around. Every single one of the buggers. Only one other person would appreciate the irony and I rang Jo, my eldest daughter, in San Francisco, and as I expected her reaction was sheer hilarity.

'You really are the end, Mum. I mean I slaved for six months in a fucking income tax office to earn money to get here, took trains all the way and what happens? I walk down the road and there's your blasted picture all over the front page and looking more like my sister than my mum, you rotten cow.' You could tell she had learned her command of the English language at her mother's knee.

Associated Press had picked up the story, a coup that I guessed would cause trouble at the mill. I checked with New York and was right. The *Daily Express* had blown a gasket and there was a sharp reminder that my contract excluded me from working for anyone else. Lying through my teeth I told them I had to stay on for a few more days.

12:
19 November
Macon,
Georgia

ACON, GEORGIA, IS A BEAUTIFUL TOWN, GIVEN TO
MAGNIFICENT SKIES. At sunset it looks like an 18th
century watercolour with its ornate turrets and pedimented
buildings dating back to the War of Independence. Essentially a
colonial town, the twin of Macon in France, its foundations are
in freemasonry. There is an elk, a moose or a buffalo in front of
many of the white-painted, porticoed, clapboard buildings. The
streets are wide, the civic buildings solid and architecturally
handsome, upholding traditional standards. Traditions like the
divine right of money, white superiority and the right to carry
a gun. These virtues are counter-balanced by a humorous
tolerance of dotty moonshiners belting about the countryside in
battered Dodge trucks. The blacks, who outnumber the whites
by eight to one, are also tolerated, just so long as they stick to

the menial jobs like sweeping the streets. Macon has a high crime rate. Most of the crimes are domestic. The combination of readily available wood-alcohol and guns can be relied on to provide the police with plenty of Friday-night activity.

On Tuesday morning, my head was grateful for the crisp autumn breeze and the walk was welcome exercise after the pent-up tension of the previous few days. The main street was decorated for Thanksgiving and Christmas and I regarded the garlands with awe. I was very lucky to be seeing Christmas this year. I thought of my children waiting for news of my return, knowing that their mum would never let them down at Christmas time. I imagined their sick dread when each day passed and I did not return. It was like looking back from the grave. For the first time I began to appreciate the danger I had been in.

I found myself outside Bibb County Jail. There seemed no reason not to give it another try. Even if I was no longer a witness I could tell them I was covering the case for the English newspapers. Ron Angel was standing in the wide reception area surrounded by reporters. When I walked in the expression on his face was like that of a baritone reaching for a lower note; dislike for the world in general was his key, the press strained his range and with me he hit bottom. He looked at me with as much pleasure as he would a dog turd on the sole of his shoe.

'I have no information for you, Miss Fawkes. You will get no information from us at all.' He turned on his heel and left me standing there. I turned to one of the reporters.

'What's going on, have they found them yet?'

'No,' he said, 'they haven't. There's a huge search underway but Knowles still isn't talking.' They moved away from me, looking a little shifty. Quite right, I was contaminated and being seen talking to me would do them no good.

Right, I thought, as I walked back to the Hilton, there are 149 sources of information under this very roof. Someone is bound to talk to me and I knew the best place to find him. My voice rang out with my order. I stressed my English accent and I was very soon the centre of attention. The front page picture had done its work. The man who joined me was big, not with the fossilised weight of middle age, but tall and broad like an athlete. He was youngish, in his early 30s, with dark wavy hair and a friendly, relaxed manner that seemed to understand my mortification and make light of it. A professor of criminology at Georgia University, he was here for the conference and was fascinated by my escape, convinced that the gallows humour of the drive had contributed to my survival. He understood completely my desire to see Knowles.

'Hey, there's a reception here tonight, at the hotel. Why don't you come to it? You can be my guest, there'll be plenty to drink and maybe we can get to the sheriff and persuade him to let you see Knowles.'

'Do you think I should? A hundred and fifty sheriffs... I shouldn't think I'm very popular with people like that.'

'Sure you should, I'll introduce you to people, we'll get you your story. These guys are nice enough; they've got their wives or their girlfriends along; they're just here to enjoy themselves.'

'OK, if you say so. Where shall we meet?'

'I'll stand outside and wait for you, around 7.30 pm.' I have always maintained that a good-looking man is a more flattering accessory to a woman than a mink coat and by now enough of my self-assurance had returned for me to tart myself up in a blue lamé jacket and black satin pants. His approval of my appearance was all that I needed to brave the party. The elevators gave me a foretaste of what awaited me. They were jam-packed with robust men with iron-grey short back and sides, ladies with crimped hair, corseted torsos and pink or blue-rimmed glasses. As we were walking through the hotel lobby, I noticed the reporter I had spoken to earlier at the jail leaving the telephone in a big hurry.

'What's happening?' I asked as he dashed past.

'They've arrested Yavitz,' he shouted. 'Contempt of court. He refused to produce the tapes.' The case of Paul John Knowles was getting more complicated by the hour. The reception was a babble of old friends greeting each other, 'How ya doin'?' echoing on all sides. Glasses were being emptied at a speed that would have had even the most thoroughly-trained journalists prostrate under the table. The fruitlessness of the three-county search for the two missing men cast no detectable pall over the proceedings. The professor was as good as his word and I soon discovered that far from being a pariah I was practically the heroine of the moment. Mostly the sheriffs fussed around me, complimenting me on my escape, though I was paranoid enough to notice the few who turned heel.

The sheriff of Whitfield County, a tall, spare man with a grey crew-cut that looked as if it had just received an electric shock, introduced me as 'the little girl who helped catch Knowles,' an exaggeration I was tempted to believe until I mentioned that I would like to meet the sheriff of Bibb County. One of the party hurried away to find him. Watching out of the corner of my eye I saw him walk towards me and then stop dead six feet away. He was one of the men who had sat at the table during my first encounter with the Macon mentality. A small man, respectable in horn-rimmed glasses, the expression on his face was impassive. My new friends did their best but he refused adamantly to talk to me.

By now half the party were leaving and the other half were becoming unsteady on their feet. One in particular, with whom I had had an earnest conversation about his English ancestors and distant relatives in Chelsea, was swaying like a single stalk of wheat in a field. We were by the door, on our way to dinner, when he called out.

'Sandy, I want to make a speech, and I want everyone to listen.' He cleared a circular space on the floor. 'I think we should all thank you for what you have done, for helping the police and for helping us to catch one of the worst killers this state has known. Come on everybody, I want a round of applause for Sandy.' I felt my spine blush as the obedient hands smacked together in modest reply to the order. The drunken old fool had completely undone the diffident, apologetic but charming act I had been performing for the last hour. Sheriff Bloodworth had all the confirmation he needed, I was a publicity-seeking broad.

'That's done it,' I muttered to the professor. 'I'll never get to him now, not if they think I'm making claims like that. I had better try and retrieve what I can.' I walked across to the sheriff, displaying my good English manners. 'I am terribly sorry about that. I don't think he is very sober but I never even thought like that. I know it's not true and I am very embarrassed.'

His Southern good manners did not extend to getting up from his seat. Swivelling round, summoning from somewhere not too deep a true snarl, he said: 'I don't know what you are doing here, Miss Fawkes. You shouldn't have been allowed in. But I'll tell you, you do anything more and I'll put you in jail. It'll be a pleasure.' A vindictive-looking blonde on his right nodded in agreement. Christ, I was right up to the nostrils again.

'Somehow I don't think I won that round,' I said over dinner. 'Surely they can't put me in jail? I mean I haven't done anything. You know, I came here to learn about America and what I've learnt really scares me. Their mentality belongs somewhere back in the Dark Ages.'

'Well this is the backwoods, Sandy. It's moonshine country; most of the killings they get are domestic, or knifings in bars. They don't often get a case like this.' The sheriff of Whitfield was sitting with his wife and some friends at the next table and, over the wine, the conversation grew friendly. I told them the terrible jokes I had made about Knowles being another Boston Strangler. The women looked at me as if I was something from another planet but they weren't hostile. I pulled out all the stories about Buckingham Palace, Nureyev and the film stars I had met and was beginning to feel quite

164

smart again when the headwaiter came across to our table and told me that two men wanted to see me outside. Smart-ass became an instant jelly-fish. So the sheriff had meant what he said. He had gone straight back to his office and found some reason to put me inside.

My immediate reaction was to run away. I had to get to a phone before they took me away. Thinking that the men would be waiting for me outside the hotel, I excused myself from the table, got out of the restaurant and was making a dash for the lifts when two pairs of arms grabbed me. I was so frightened I still tried to run. If I could get to the reception desk I could tell them who to ring. But they were fast and grabbed me again. Aware that people were turning to stare, I stopped and took refuge in indignation.

'Let me go, you've got no right to arrest me! I'm British.' Up the Empire, pukka sahibs, the sovereignty of the Queen and the right of the English to wander the world unmolested – a bit out of date but it's stopped natives before now. The two men looked at me as if I was daft. One of them had a piece of yellow paper in his hand.

'You Sandra Fawkes?' I thought of saying no, then recognised that the notoriety I had been enjoying minutes before would soon put an end to such a ruse. I nodded.
'You are to appear before the grand jury at 9.30 am tomorrow.'

'I don't know what you are talking about, I haven't done anything wrong.' I looked at the paper. It was terrifying. There was my name. I was being summoned by the United States. The men obviously had no idea why I was in such a state of panic.

They didn't know that the grand jury and the Inquisition were welded in my mind, that I thought I was going to be sentenced the following day for some crime known only to them. I was totally unfamiliar with the processes of American law, but I did know that people were jailed for crimes they hadn't committed and let out 20 years later to prove their innocence. Films had seen to my education. Looking totally baffled by my agitation, the two men said goodnight and left.

I dashed upstairs and phoned the *Daily Express* to tell them that I had been arrested. It was 5.00 am in London and only the dogwatch was on duty, but the man at the other end was a friend and he too was surprised at my state. To him I was their girl in the field who never missed a deadline, always got the job done. He had no idea of the depth of my ignorance.

'It's just a formality, Sandy. They want you to register some information, it's nothing to get in a stew about, goes on all the time.'

'But they arrested the lawyer,' I protested. 'He's in jail right now. God, if I ever get out of this I'll never talk to strange men again!' We chatted for a while about my adventure. He found me the number of the British Consul in Atlanta and that of the local stringer – just in case any strings needed to be pulled. I received the comforting news that I was the talk of Fleet Street and then I was alone again, the umbilical cord to the office severed. Still unsure, I decided to return to the dining-room and consult the experts. The professor had left, but the sheriff of Whitfield was still there dispensing Southern hospitality and he confirmed that the yellow paper did not mean that I was under arrest, merely subpoenaed. My frayed nerves were indebted to him and the generous brandies ensured a good night's sleep. There was no time to think that this time last week I had been playing sulky games with a man whose rage could wreck a room, who had killed 12 strangers, people he didn't even dislike, a man who was now sleeping in a cell approximately 200 yards away.

By the morning, rain was lashing at the windows. The last leaves on the trees no longer clung to life and were sailing madly down the torrential gutters. Winter had arrived. The two missing men didn't stand much chance of staying alive in weather like that. They had now been out in the open for three days and three bitter nights. That day was the start of the quail-hunting season and the search would have the additional help of 500 amateurs. It would be their last chance.

The grand jury hearing was to be held in the old Post Office building, an imposing grey stone edifice set back from the wide sidewalk, with one of those long flights of shallow steps so familiar from countless courtroom dramas. Even the big black man indolently redistributing the grime on the end of a vast broom-shaped mop, dressed in ill-fitting overalls and shoes that gaped beyond his heels, looked like a fictional character, an extra playing some Minstrel stereotype character.

My heart was beating as frantically as the quails' as I walked down the marble corridors to the room marked US Attorney, Public, in gold Roman lettering on sanded glass. Jess Branson of WBML was lounging in front of a desk. I had rung him earlier to say I couldn't make the radio show and the sight of him was as welcome as a glass of water in the desert. He introduced me to the secretary, who was chatty and hospitable with coffee and the information that I would be paid a few dollars a day for my services as a witness. It wasn't the money so much as being back on the right side of the law that comforted me. I still didn't know much about what was going on.

Through the open door came a young man of such incredibly good looks I began to cheer up immediately. He asked me to step into his office, a room lined from wall to wall with leather-bound books. Reference books, I supposed, but they could have been bought by the yard for all the handling they seemed to have received. He sat behind a mahogany desk of patriarchal proportions and introduced himself. He was Tom Vockrodt, Special Attorney to the United States Department of Justice. He looked awfully young for the job, particularly behind that desk. It took me about three seconds to decide to throw myself on his mercy. Some decisions are harder than others.

He explained to me that the reason I had to give official evidence was that Knowles's lawyer had refused to hand over the secret tapes and, since my signed statement in Florida had led them to believe that the tapes might contain information on various crimes they were investigating, cases which involved several states, the Federal Bureau of Investigation wanted affirmation of their existence. He looked even more impressive when I knew he was working for the FBI. I answered the same old questions: Was Knowles a homosexual? Had I slept with him? Where had I met him? As I handed out the sordid details I felt like Orpheus watching Eurydice disappear, for the man opposite me, so tall and blond, wearing a Shetland wool, herringbone tweed suit cut to conceal his healthy frame and a button-down Viyella shirt, was all that Knowles was not, could never have been. Knowles had thought that the acquisition of a chic car, credit cards and stylish clothes would take him out of the working class he was born into, but it couldn't. The Holiday Inn was the height of his aspirations. The man in the bar who had said he was a redneck had been right. And I was no better; I had mistaken money and a flash and fashionable style for class. The real thing, Yale, Harvard or whatever, was sitting in front of me.

It was not a good moment, and it was the first of several to be endured that morning. There was a picture in the outer room, the Statue of Liberty surrounded by mist and choppy sea. I was to become as familiar with that picture as if I were painting it by numbers. The wheels of the law turn slowly for the innocent, and the hours of waiting were tedious. The papers that day carried an interview with Angela Covic, a girl from San Francisco. She was the girl who had helped Knowles to gain his parole earlier in the year, in May.

They first came into contact in two years previously as pen pals through a magazine called *American Astrology*. Knowles was in jail. She liked the look of his handwriting and the correspondence flourished. She told him of her marital difficulties, he told her that he was inside having been busted for drugs, that he had been in a pop group playing trumpet and guitar. He called her his Yiddisher Angel and decorated his letters with crayonned drawings of flowers, astral symbols and

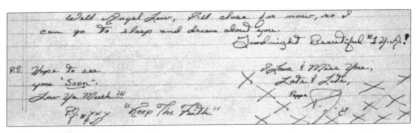

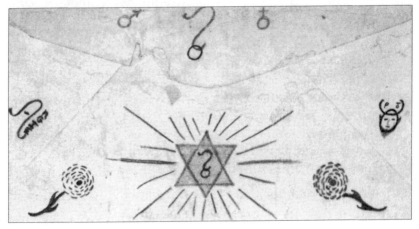

Above: Excerpt from a letter to Angela Covic, written by Knowles while in prison.

Below: The envelope, decorated with symbols in coloured crayon.

rather jolly-looking devils with his initials, PJ, between the horns. The letters made no mention of his career in petty crime. Angela's mother was a psychic and Angela went to one of their psychic friends for advice as the letters became more frequent and more loving. The friend advised Angela to get a lawyer and to try to get Knowles out of jail before Christmas the previous year.

Angela travelled to Raiford Penitentiary that September to meet Knowles for the first time. They decided then that they would marry as soon as he was free. She went to Miami and met Sheldon Yavitz through mutual friends. He set about organising the parole on technical terms. While she was in Miami, she went to another psychic woman who told her that she had a very dangerous man around her. She was on sufficiently bad terms with her husband at the time to think the reference was to him. Her mother paid the lawyer's bill and Yavitz had no idea that Angela knew nothing of Knowles's past. It must have seemed like salvation to Knowles – a real chance to start a new life. Angela had even prepared a job for him; on the strength of his handwriting and the decorations on the letters she had persuaded a sign-writer in San Francisco to give him a job.

Christmas came and went, and still Yavitz had not managed to secure his parole. It came finally on 14 May. Angela sent him his airfare but, when he turned up on the doorstep of her house overlooking the Bay of San Francisco, she was uneasy.

'I just had a funny feeling about him, I didn't want anything to do with him,' she said in the interview. 'I guess it was intuition. He stayed round the house for four days but I made him sleep at my mother's, she liked him, but he never did go after the job.' And after those four days Angela asked him to leave, told him she didn't want to marry him after all. She put him on a plane back to Jacksonville. Soon after that she and her husband Bob were reconciled.

Knowles phoned her again in September. He was on the West Coast and wanted to see her. She told him she was back with Bob and didn't want to see him. The next time Knowles rang her husband answered. He had rung again just the previous Friday evening saying he was in trouble, but she had been unable to help. The following day she had received a card from him saying, 'Surprise... I'm still alive. PJ.'

It was from the Hotel Fontainbleu, Miami. Her intuition had been sharper than mine. Also in the newspaper, among the news of the state Governor's intention to run for the presidency, a woman who beat her child to death and the sentencing of two young airmen who had held up a music shop and forced five customers to drink drain cleaner before shooting them all, was an amusing little picture. It showed Sheriff Bloodworth, all dressed up for the party, standing outside the maximum-security cell and demonstrating that Knowles had no chance of escape. Self-conscious and erect for the photographer, he almost managed a smile. So did I.

You enter the court through solid mahogany doors that are 14-foot high. They are enough to put the fear into God himself as they swing open. There was plenty going on behind them while I waited outside for my turn. I was kept up to date by local journalists. Despite his night in the clink, Sheldon Yavitz was unbowed and he once again refused to obey judge Wilbur Owen's order to hand over the tapes. Although admitting to the court that they might be pertinent to the Milledgeville murders, the only case with which Knowles had so far been charged, he added that the tapes were incriminating beyond the jurisdiction of the Georgia court and involved Knowles's activities throughout the United States. The reporters were now telling me gleefully that Knowles could have killed as many as 25 people. Judge Owens ordered two marshals to escort Yavitz to his home in Miami and search the place.

At lunchtime I was given another subpoena to appear the following day. I was also told that Knowles was being arraigned at Milledgeville that afternoon. Professional interest suggested I should go there, but the suggestion was firmly rejected. I could not face going to the place where Mandy Carr had been killed; her mother might even be at the court. I couldn't cope with that. By now I didn't even want to see Knowles, I was a bystander in a sickening story and the sooner I got myself out the better.

I was sitting alone in my room watching the clouds racing against the sullen orange sunset when the phone rang. It was Yavitz's wife, Patsy, downstairs in the foyer. I had seen her earlier outside the courtroom, a sparkly girl with dark plaits gathered in bunches either side of her head. She looked as out of place in Macon as I felt. Her company was very welcome, indeed just to talk to a woman after the last few days would be a relief. She too was going quietly out of her mind. Macon was as foreign to her as it was to me; she desperately needed to talk. She acted as Sheldon's secretary and had come on the journey to give him support, leaving her three children behind in the care of the housekeeper. The youngest one was only a few months old. Now she too had been subpoenaed for the next day. We were both scared.

She had never met Knowles, never even seen him. Shelley, as she called Yavitz, had made sure he didn't come to the house. Her 12-year-old son had met him briefly and had been dreadfully upset at the weekend to learn that the nice man was wanted for murder. I told her of the weekend, the waiting and the lost phone calls, how I wished I had been able to get in touch with them. We went on to discuss Knowles's character, why he had suddenly turned killer. Was it the rejection in San Francisco? All the murders stemmed from last July.

'I think he just wanted to be somebody important,' Patsy said simply. 'That's why he arranged the tapes and the will, so that anything from it would go to his mother; his family would be rich.' She paused and looked at me. 'You know, he told Shelley he was longing to tell you the truth, he had a great respect for you and liked you a lot.'

'Just as well in the circumstances,' I laughed. 'I still go through the horrors, thinking of the number of opportunities he had to kill me. I could be anywhere, I would never have been found, my children would have had to go through the rest of their lives not knowing what happened to me. It's ghastly, ghastly. Do you know, they even thought I was part of it at one time.' And out it all poured, the interrogations, the insinuations and the awful moment when I had recognised Carswell Carr's bright yellow blazer. The moment I *knew*.

'And then I saw the pictures, the pictures of the bodies. That poor little kid. He had stuffed her tights –pantyhose, you call them – right down her throat. He had tied her up and raped her. Poor, poor little soul.' Patsy told me that Ellis Rubin, Yavitz's lawyer and mentor, was flying in the next morning. Rubin was very famous, she said, he had defended the Cubans in the Watergate affair. Once again I felt my ignorance. I didn't even know lawyers had lawyers. There certainly was a lot to learn about America.

Later that day I had a call from the FBI. They wanted to know if I had talked to Patsy Yavitz. On impulse I denied it. Later, I tried to work out why. I was confused. I didn't seem to know which side I was on. Indeed it was hard at times to work out which side was which. Like so many things in this country, American justice was totally foreign and utterly incomprehensible to me. When it had been simply the police hunting a suspected murderer, things had been relatively clear. Now the lawyers had arrived and the picture was becoming murky. I had two sides, too. The girl guide in me, the side that said, 'Tell the truth, and nothing but the truth,' had got me into trouble from the moment I had owned up to screwing Knowles. Then there was the other side, the greedy side, the part of me that wanted to write the book.

I wrote myself a severe reprimand on standards but decided to do nothing, to play both sides of the fence. The way I had been treated in Macon, I owed the buggers nothing, and if I played the FBI informer I might be forced to divulge the tantalizing titbit Patsy had given me. She had told me that the marshals had no chance of finding the tapes: they were hidden in a safe behind a picture in her housekeeper's part of the house. The account to come out of Miami about the events of that afternoon would say that when the marshals arrived with Yavitz, the housekeeper had barred them from her rooms behind the garage. 'I ain't a part of this thing,' she was reported as saying. Her rooms were the only ones in the house that the marshals didn't search during their four-hour stay. Had Patsy picked up the phone and tipped her off about the impending search? I was not about to sever all connections with the story by telling everything I knew.

It was cocktail hour, the pianist was smiling and playing good jazz and when he joined me at the bar we talked about old-fashioned music and men like Sydney Bechet, Johnny Dodds and Frankie Trambauer, a sweet change from the horror movie I was living. Sitting in bars gives me no pain, even when I am alone. I like to look at people, watch tentative love affairs blossom under Bacchus' glow, see the spite in married couples when the spirits get them, listen to the infinite tedium of men telling other men how they train their 'dawgs' to recognise the sound of their tyres turning into the drive. The boredom and isolation of a crowded bar is soothing.

My solitary drinking was interrupted by a couple of phone calls. One was from a woman journalist trying to trap me into admitting that Knowles was the great romance of my life; very short shrift she received. As I was returning to the bar a man left his table and came up to me. He warned me that I was being watched by the police. Unobtrusively, he pointed out a heavy-set man at the other end of the bar who had followed me to the phone booth for each call. My benefactor said he did not like to think of such things happening in his city. I thanked him and left for my room, once again furious and thoroughly frightened. Would this ordeal never end? I felt as Knowles must have done: hunted, but ignorant of where or how the trap would fall.

I determined to outwit my persecutors and, taking the lift to the basement car park, crept out into the street, not caring where I went just so long as *they* didn't know. It had been raining again and the glistening streets were utterly deserted. My footsteps grated as I ground the gravel from nearby roadworks beneath my feet. The sky was pitch black and the sound of the wind in the trees was suddenly ominous, carrying on it images of death and desolation. The walk began to seem like a mistake, a foolish gesture. I turned into the first motel I came to and ordered a taxi.

That night I wrote myself another note: 'I must pull myself together and remember the promise I made to myself at 15, never, ever again to be frightened of anyone.' I had just won a scholarship to art school and with it freedom forever from the people who had always treated me as someone tainted and degraded because I was illegitimate. My independence had been hard-won; this was no time for slipping back. On Thursday morning the courtroom was bustling. Ellis Rubin had arrived on the 8.30 am plane and his wiry, energetic elegance proved a rich contrast to the locals in their dark, synthetic suits with narrow lapels and trousers deliberately shortened to reveal inches of brightly coloured sock. The jury, six men, one of Asian descent, and six women including a raven-haired gum-chewer, looked overawed by the courtroom which was as lofty as its intentions. The judge sat on high, his chiselled face weary with the solemnity of his task. Reporters came in and out for whispered conferences. Tom Vockrodt stood there looking unhappy, but very sure of himself. No smart aleck lawyer from Miami was going to outwit the power of the United States.

Ellis Rubin began by announcing that his client would plead the Fifth Amendment if she was asked questions that were injurious to her husband. Patsy affirmed that her husband had received into his custody on 25 October certain objects from Paul John Knowles and that, as she knew the contents might be incriminating to him, she would not reveal the whereabouts of the safe. The judge threatened her with a charge of contempt of court, the same charge that had led her husband to a night in jail, but she still refused on the grounds that she was protected both as a wife and as her husband's secretary. An adjournment was sought and refused. The judge then offered her a private conference in chambers but Rubin turned it down.

Judge Wilbur Owens leaned forward in his chair and looked hard at Patsy Yavitz standing there in her braids and short, check jacket. Then he turned to Ellis Rubin, his flat vowels sonorous. 'I am holding her for contempt. I wonder what her attitude would be if her husband was missing out there. She has not given a thought to the wife of that State Trooper. She might find out she could have saved a man's life and she will have to live with that knowledge till her doomsday.' I was very glad I had kept my mouth shut. It seemed that here even the judges believed in Judgement Day! Then Ellis Rubin spoke to a couple of reporters outside, acknowledging that he knew where the safe was and within moments subpoenas were flying around like confetti. I was led to another room to wait my turn. Two other people were there already, Ron Angel and a tiny woman in a miniskirt and a glossy black beehive wig. The face below the mass of hair had been dealt with unkindly by the years. I guessed that she must be Jackie Knight, the girlfriend from Macon. I introduced myself.

'Yes, I know who you are. Paul told me about you. You are the one who is going to write the book.'

'Well, I'd like to, but I can't get in to see him. Have you seen him again?'

'Yes, but he won't talk about anything, just makes jokes.' Her eyes were tired with too many years of problems, but she looked up and said, strongly and loyally, 'I don't believe he done it. Nobody who knows him believes he could do a thing like that, not to a 15-year-old girl. My daughter is 15 and he worshipped her, I'm sure he didn't do it.' There was nothing to say. I couldn't tell her I had seen the evidence, had even worn the watch. Let her believe a little longer. She would find out soon enough. The headlines now claimed that Knowles might have killed as many as 25 people.

The papers also printed the alleged agreement between

Yavitz and Knowles. It purported to state that Yavitz would hold in trust certain recordings, documents, manuscripts, writings, memos, so provided and created by Knowles. That the items would from time to time be forwarded to the attorney, sealed and not to be opened until Knowles's death or upon written authorization. Knowles's will directed Yavitz to 'make my life story, record, and history known to the world and for the good of society.' It went on to mention 'books, movies, television' and other media for disseminating Knowles's story.

In court, Yavitz had said that Knowles had told him that two slayings in Milledgeville and nine felonies in Florida were discussed on tapes. Knowles must have spent the day I met him recording the Carr murders on the equipment he had bought at Zayre's on Carswell Carr's credit card. He must have posted the tape immediately, because I never once saw him with a package. Jackie's story was in the papers too. She had met Knowles in Jacksonville seven years earlier when he was 21 and just out of prison. Her husband, a musician, had introduced them. She had felt sorry for him.

'He felt he was an outcast,' she said. The Knights invited him to their home and he soon became a family friend. He was devoted to her three children and whenever there was a fair locally would take them, winning prizes and presents for them. Soon afterwards he was in trouble again and back in prison. While he was there, Jackie's marriage broke up. She began to write to Paul and visit him and, in the loneliness of bringing up three small children, the friendship turned into romance. Knowles took a correspondence course to improve himself, learned to be a welder and wrote to Jackie proposing marriage. She had worked all her life, he said, and now he wanted to look after her so that she could stay at home with her children. He was going to go straight. High hopes but no opportunities. He was paroled in but found the prison tag was always with him; no one wanted to employ an ex-convict. Paul drifted back to his drinking mates and he and Jackie broke up.

'I loved him,' she said, 'but I had a feeling he was going back to prison.' Not long after Jackie moved her family to Macon, Paul John Knowles was in custody again. Jackie eventually married another man but that too didn't last. She had been up since 5.00 am earning enough money for her family as a waitress in a roadside restaurant.

Paul visited her whenever he was in the area. He had popped in sometime during August to give her a portable colour television set. She had a shrewd idea he hadn't bought it and she was right. The FBI had been round to her house to collect it. It had belonged to a woman in Atlantic Beach, a suburb of Jacksonville. She had been murdered on 2 August. He had been staying with Jackie early in November and for the first time she had felt uncomfortable with him. He had left the house late on the evening of 5 November and she had seen him again in the morning. She was relieved to find him gone when she returned from work. It was a sad story but a classic one, the sort that had led William B Saxbe to conclude that prison was the only place for criminals, that parole did no good.

Before we returned to court, I had a quick conference with Tom Vockrodt and told him in no uncertain terms that I was not going to have my relationship with Knowles made public. The situation I was in was fraught enough; owning up to bedding a mass murderer in a town that was waiting for the Day of Judgement was more than I was prepared to risk. If he asked me any personal questions I would refuse to testify. Last night's lecture had worked.

At 5.00 pm, as we were settling down in court, the news broke. Charles E Campbell and James E Meyer had been found. They had been tied to a tree and shot in the back of the head. They had been found by deer hunters in a dense thicket of pines in Pulaski County, about 40 miles south of Macon. The hunters could see no sign of a struggle but the men had obviously been dead several days. Campbell's revolver was missing. Georgia Public Safety Commissioner Herman Cofer, who had been in charge of the search, told the press that Knowles had said that one word would give them the clue to the hostages' where-abouts, but he had refused to give it. The word was Pabst. There was a Pabst brewery near where they were found. Knowles was playing his power game to the hilt.

And enjoying his notoriety. The papers were filled with pictures of his appearance at Milledgeville and accounts of his behaviour. The streets had been lined with people. Sightseers had hung over the sides of balconies to catch a glimpse of Knowles, manacled and in leg irons, dressed in a brilliant orange jumpsuit. He had loved it: the local co-eds four deep on the sidewalks, the courtroom packed with reporters, friends, Mandy's school chums and relatives of the Carr family. It was an event, he was the centre of it and he smiled at everyone. No wonder he had laughed like a hyena at his capture; he was having his hour of glory, not in the hereafter as he had predicted, but in the here-and-now. The daily stories of the women in his life had turned him into a Casanova killer, a folk villain, Dillinger and Jesse James rolled into one. The long years of failure, loneliness and rejection were over. He had an identity now. He was already being referred to as the most heinous killer in history.

Alongside the stories ran the news that Debbie Griffin's purse had been found near the spot where her boyfriend's body had been discovered on 15 November. The couple had been hitchhiking from Gainesville, Florida to Love Valley, North Carolina, when they disappeared. They had last been seen on 2 November. Edward Hillard had been shot five times. His girlfriend's jeans and jacket were found nearby, but her body had disappeared. As the press delighted in pointing out, Knowles was known to have been in the area on 2 November.

On the 12th floor of the Macon Hilton, a Feydeau farce was in progress. Tom Vockrodt and Joe Cavallas of the FBI were in rooms along the corridor from me. Ellis Rubin and his wife had the room opposite. To find out what was going on without using the phones was a matter of peering round the door, listening to check that the elevator wasn't coming, then bolting frantically into each other's rooms. One minute I was pounding on Tom's door saying that the Atlanta papers had told me there was a warrant out for my arrest for receiving stolen property, the next I was sneaking into the Rubins' room to find out what was going on in Miami. We were all awash with subpoenas and orders to appear at various offices and courts and no-one had a clear idea of what was going on. I had given up all thought of booking on the 4.30 pm flight out. The way things were going I could be there till the trial.

Another Thursday evening. Would I ever rid my mind of that moment two weeks before when I had discarded the Gideon Bible for the bar, or the eager look on his face as he walked up and asked me to dance? I knew now that at that moment as he came towards me, clean and shining, I was to have been the next victim. It was my ability to write – and to laugh – that had saved me. I ordered another drink. The bar at the Hilton was as gloomy as I felt. Tom Vockrodt and Joe Cavallas walked in and my heart sank, more trouble.

'Ah, we were looking for you.'

'What have I done now?'

'Nothing. We came to take you out to dinner. We thought you were having such an awful time we'd better do something to cheer you up.' For the first time that week I felt like a human being. Fancy the FBI caring how I felt, or was it a trap? Oh well, if it was, it was an extremely handsome one and so long as I forgot about Patsy's safe I could keep out of trouble. We talked about the case and Tom told me I had no chance of seeing Knowles, the GBI would make sure of that. They were as fond of me as I was of them. They weren't too keen on the Miami contingent either, it seemed.

I asked Tom about the trial. When would it be? Would I have to come back for it? He looked thoughtfully into his beer. 'There may not be a trial.'

'What do you mean?'

'Knowles may plead guilty, then you wouldn't have to come back. Then again he could plead insanity.'

'It looks to me as if he is determined to get as much notoriety out of the case as he can,' I said, referring to the smiling photographs that had knocked the story of a major fatal aircrash off the front pages.

'Yes,' said Tom grimly, 'but I wouldn't rely on coming back.' A dark thought crossed my mind but I dismissed it immediately. The days of the lynch mob were over, even in the South.

We went on to discuss politics and the law. They were highly amused at my image of the grand jury. Joe had been one of the man who had presented me with the subpoena and had wondered then why I was in such a panic. I told him of Sheriff Bloodworth's threat and he understood my fears. I thanked Tom for his handling of my hearing; it had gone very smoothly and the judge had been most courteous.

'How much longer do you think you will be keeping me here?' I asked them. I knew I had another court appearance to make but no definite date had been set.

'It's difficult to tell,' said Tom casually. 'It all depends on when we get hold of those tapes.' Ah. Was this the trap? I thought of my conversation with Patsy, of Patsy sitting at this moment in a cell round the corner and debated what to do. Bide my time and get off the subject, I decided. We ended the evening with a splendidly fierce and partisan argument about the merits of British and American newspapers.

When I got back to my room I was still pondering the dilemma of the tapes. Thinking it all over yet again I decided to wait and see. If Yavitz and Rubin invited me to write the book I would keep quiet; if not I would spill the lot and go home on Monday. The girl guide could go underground for a bit. I was not responsible for anybody's death, I told myself. My life was the one that had been at risk. A mirage of money, the great corrupter, was vivid before my eyes.

Events sometimes save our souls and mine was saved the following day. Yavitz was presented with the choice of his wife and himself staying in jail until the court forgave his contempt or directing the Florida marshals to the hidden safe and giving them the combination. He argued at length but finally agreed to write down the directions and the combination. If Patsy had not been with him he would probably have sat it out until he could appeal to a higher court. Judge Owens made it clear that he alone would listen to the tapes and would decide their future. As the lawyers bluffed and double-bluffed each other, the fact that Knowles was a killer seemed to diminish in importance. The law became more important than the innocent lives he had taken, the grief and misery he had caused in his bid for fame. The law was a game of chess and Knowles had merely set up the pieces.

The day passed in endless waiting. I discovered Ron Angel talking to Jackie, concerned about the hideous gossip she was receiving from her neighbours. He even talked to me, pointing to a club across the road where Little Richard had been discovered, laughing a little at the make-up he had worn. Ron Angel fascinated me. I watched him at every opportunity. In the pictures with Knowles when they were handcuffed together, one might have thought Angel was the criminal, his cropped head was so bowed. His politeness fitted him like the iron band round a barrel of explosives. He called everyone sir or ma'am, but he never looked at ease. He seemed to trust no one and applied himself to his work with solid devotion, seeing everything and saying little. He frightened me.

At 5.30 pm on Friday 22 November, Sheldon Yavitz was in court to see US Marshals Ed Stout from Miami and Bob Hall from Macon hand over two sealed packages to judge Owens. They had been discovered in a two-ton desk-size safe in the housekeeper's room, behind a wall hanging. Judge Owens showed his gratitude for Yavitz's co-operation by putting him on bail for $30,000 till the following Wednesday, when he would have to show the court why he should not be held in criminal contempt for not producing the tapes when first ordered. Yavitz actually laughed in the judge's face. There he was, sitting up on high, asking a man from another state to raise a preposterous sum of money on a Friday afternoon. Yavitz had no choice but to spend the next five days in jail; Patsy had been released that morning. They were like a pair of weathercocks.

Ellis Rubin and his assistant, Charles Marchman from Macon, petitioned to have Yavitz's subpoena quashed, quoting the Fourth Amendment to the United States Constitution which grants the attorney-client privilege. They also argued that Yavitz was protected by the Fifth and Fourteenth Amendments which stipulate that a person may not be required to give incriminating evidence against himself and that this includes information an attorney obtains from his client. Judge Wilbur Owens was implacable. The petitions were denied in seconds.

'Let the record reflect that two US Marshals delivered to this judge two packages,' was all he would say. He wasn't even having it on record that the packages contained the Knowles tapes. Ellis Rubin had no alternative but to appeal to a higher court. Outside he was quoted as saying he was 'going back to the United States for the weekend'. He meant good old, sophisticated Miami.

On the same day, the Governor of Georgia appointed the State Attorney-General to assist in the prosecution of Paul John Knowles on numerous charges. Two cities from the State of Florida had asked for murder charges to be filed against Knowles. One was for the strangling of Mrs Marjorie Howie of Atlantic Beach. The killer had taken a portable colour TV set from the dead woman's apartment. The other was in connection with the death of Mrs Alice Curtis, an elderly schoolteacher from Jacksonville. The report said she had been choked to death and that her car had been found in Lima, Ohio. She had been killed on 27 July, the credit cards of William Bates, from Lima, Ohio, missing since 3 September, had been used in 25 different states. The trail of violence was growing longer. In the paper that day, Knowles was quoted as saying that he was the only 'successful' member of his family.

I had been graciously allowed to leave town for the weekend. Needless to say, permission had come through two hours after the last plane had left Macon. I shared a car to the airport on Saturday morning with Ellis Rubin and his wife Irene. We were all a little elated and of course Knowles was our sole topic of conversation. Rubin had gathered from Yavitz that Knowles had enjoyed the killings, was proud of his achievement. He had become a proficient, professional killer and was incapable of relating to his victims.

'Did Yavitz know that those two men, the hostages, were dead? Did he know where they were?'

Rubin shrugged. His eyes were candid, hard. 'Who knows?' he said. They were catching a plane to Miami; I was heading back to West Palm Beach, to the kind of people who would do anything to beat you to a story, bore the arse off you, rant, scream and rave, but would never, ever put a woman through the week Mrs Charles Campbell and her two children had been through. My friends were wonderful, flawed human beings and I was thankful to be returning to them. The flight was the one I should have caught those two long weeks ago, the 10.20 am from Atlanta. Two weeks ago Knowles had torn out the front page of the *Atlanta Constitution*; now his story was occupying the headlines every day.

High in the air, watching summer return to the landscape below, I thought of Judge Owens and didn't envy him his weekend's listening. From all accounts, Knowles hadn't made a tape recording of the actual killings, but Owens would be subjected to hours of description, recalled with pride. Thinking too of Mrs Campbell and Mrs Carr, of the other mothers, children and husbands, I began to see the reason for Macon's belligerence, why Ron Angel hated the outsiders who came in for the financial kill, myself included. It was their people who had been murdered, and the fight over the ownership of the tapes demonstrated on the simplest level that there is law and there is justice.

By Tuesday, Knowles had been ousted from the headlines by a poltergeist in Bridgeport, Connecticut, but he was still occupying a lot of space with a smiling picture, his hair longer and the dejected Angel always in the background. The crowds had been out in force again for his formal charging with the Carr murders. The kids' watch, the tuxedos, the patent shoes that had danced like Fred Astaire, the clock radio were all produced in evidence. Knowles had joined wholeheartedly in the laughter when a shopgirl who had sold him recording equipment and some tapes in Macon, a purchase paid for with Carr's credit card, identified him as being 'red-headed, fairly nice-looking and he smelt good'. I remembered that smell.

Outside the Baldwin County courtroom, the scene would have gratified a film star. Photographers and television cameramen jostled for position. He smiled for them all despite the catcalls from the crowd. No wonder Ron Angel ducked. Sheldon Yavitz had been allowed out to attend his client's hearing and was later released from custody by a three-judge panel of the US Fifth Circuit Court of Appeals. Ellis Rubin had not been lazy.

Going back to Macon after the pleasures of Florida was like being recalled to a war zone after a week in London. The day continued as badly as it started. The *Daily Express* in London was by no means pleased with my extended stay in the States. In typical newspaper fashion they had kept their communication brief.

'Who is paying, the FBI or us?' read the message that came through via New York.

I kept the reply brief, too. 'The FBI.' I dreaded to think what would happen to my career if I was remanded for the trial, but this was perhaps a healthy sign: I was now more worried about my job at home than about being accidentally shot in Macon. The stroll from the Hilton to the court had become familiar territory by now. A few people nodded and one woman stopped me on the street to say she had been part of my grand jury and that she hoped I would one day come back to Macon in happier circumstances. The black man was still redistributing the same old grime with the same old mop and we smiled. The mist had not lifted from the Statue of Liberty and my backside said hello to the hard wooden benches outside the courtroom. Jackie was there, having discarded her beehive and looking a lot better for it, despite the news that her 15-year-old daughter had run away and got married. Jackie was resigned to it, as she was by now to the fact that Paul had killed Mandy.

I slipped into the court for the hearing and felt the electric shock immediately. Knowles was there and I felt the magnetism, the power, before I saw him. He turned round at the same moment. It was the first time I had seen him since I had said such a firm goodbye in Florida and I started to shake as the old familiar horrors returned to torture me. I had to leave. I stood outside the door and knew that I wanted to put as much distance as was humanly possible between me and that evil power in there. The door opened 15 minutes later and he was led out. I was calm now, prepared, but as he passed me in the corridor there was nothing to say. We smiled. 'You look good,' he said.

And he was gone out of my life forever.

13:
18 December
Fleet Street,
London

13:
18 December,
Freet Street,
London

THE CITY GOLF CLUB IN FLEET STREET IS A
CAVERNOUS EMPORIUM SET ALONGSIDE THE CRYPT
OF ST BRIDE'S CHURCH. The church was designed by Sir
Christopher Wren in 1665 and resembles a wedding cake. It
has a handsome, secular interior and is used with sentimental
regularity for memorial services when any of the established
characters of the Street fall off the perch.

The City Golf Club, however, is used every day and there is
frequently very little difference between the rigor mortis on
either side of the wall separating the crypt from the club. To a
journalist the office is a home from home and the pub is the
office's home from home. It is not a place to go looking for a
job but it is a very good place to spend time seeking
unemployment. I had been back in London three weeks to the

day and was reporting for bar duty early. My adventures in the US, though the source of much ribaldry in the bars, had not done my career a great deal of good in the office. The new editor was not amused and my services as a writer seemed to be needed less and less.

It had been a difficult three weeks. Everyone had wanted to know the story, the number of people Knowles had killed and what he was like in bed. At home, I felt like my own ghost, touching possessions I might never have seen again, listening to music I might never have heard. The children and I hugged a lot, hovered over each other, only our eyes acknowledging what might have been. At work the incident was quickly yesterday's news, but I could sense the editor's disapproval moving through the executive echelons like the soft shuffling of cards.

The nights were the worst, the long sleepless hours of self-hatred. Over and over again I tried to come to terms with the fact that this body had lain next to that body, had been caressed by those hands, hands which found pleasure in killing. And each night was spent alone. Sensing the conflict raging within me and being unable to cope, my lovers had discarded me. Inside, I was a new person but nobody guessed. America had been my ordeal by fire and I had emerged scorched but alive and stronger. The repartee was as quick and vulgar as ever, but I still felt the presence of the dead all around me, weird and isolating. A few other early birds were in the club, debating whether to cure their hangover with a Bloody Mary or take a flyover with a bottle of champagne. When the phone rings, as it does frequently in every hostelry in the Street as editors seek out their missing reporters, the guilt is communal. Almost everyone should be elsewhere and the barmen are the best actors in the world. Holding the phone at arm's length they call out the name, usually right over the head of its owner, thus giving the reporter about 15 seconds to decide whether to own up or drink up and sneak out. When it rang that morning I knew for once that I was in the clear, so I paid no attention. But it was for me. Jill King, the deputy news editor, wanted me in the office. That was odd, I hardly ever worked for the news desk; I was on features, the lyrical word was my forte; it was well known that I was hopeless on details and always forgot to ask people their age and address. But I was getting paid and decided I had better skidaddle across the road.

Dodging between buses and taxis, I made it. The foyer, decorated in cast steel art deco murals preserved as an historical monument to the glories that were the 1930s, was filling with executives awaiting their office cars to take them to lunch at the Savoy. John MacDonald, an assistant editor who had laboured long in the early days to get my efforts into the paper, stood shrugging himself into his navy blue mac.

'They've shot your boyfriend,' he announced cheerfully. For a second I hated him. Hated the whole newspaper game where tragedy is just another headline. Even as I felt it I was ashamed. John had carried his own grief with dignity when his son had died a year previously; containing emotions was one of the rules of the game. Abiding by the rules, I smiled. 'Oh, really?' Then I fled for the lift. Upstairs I told Jill I knew; the impassive face we wear to protect ourselves was on again. I read the dispatch

'Paul John Knowles, an alleged mass-murderer suspected in at least 20 killings across the United States was shot dead in an apparent attempt to escape while being transferred from one maximum security jail to another. Dateline 18 December, Douglasville, Georgia.' I put the slip of paper down, thanked her and went to my desk. I stared blindly at the grey brick wall opposite, feeling nothing; no shock, no pity, no revenge, no elation, nothing. I sat there for hours, unwilling to face the fresh wave of interest the news would bring, needing the privacy of the empty office, knowing that the cautiously-worded letter I had delayed sending would never reach him now. I had offered him, the human being not the killer, friendship during the long years ahead. I had half expected to be called to the trial, but now it wouldn't take place. I remembered Tom Vockrodt saying at dinner, 'There may not be a trial... I wouldn't rely on coming back.' So he had been right.

Georgia has the electric chair. Paul John Knowles would almost certainly have died in it.

I was glad he was dead. It was over.

Later, I looked through my diary and counted the days. Forty. Forty days since we had sat in the Polaris lounge at the top of the Hyatt Regency Hotel in Atlanta and I had stared into those strange yellow eyes and heard him say: 'I am going to be killed. Soon. It could be in two days or two months, I don't know when, but within a year I shall be dead. I shall be killed for something I have done in the past.'

He was right. He had had 40 days to live.

A reporter from an Atlanta newspaper rang that afternoon to say that there was a huge controversy brewing over Knowles's death. Some people were saying that Knowles had been executed. What was my opinion?

'I suppose that must be anyone's immediate reaction, but I don't know the details. Tell me what happened.'

'The police here say that Knowles had volunteered to show them where he had hidden Charles Campbell's gun. He was being transferred from one jail to another and said he would show them on the way. They say that he managed to free one hand from his handcuffs and that he went for the driver's gun.'

'Can you unpick a handcuff with the police watching you all the time?'

'They found a bent paperclip under his body, they say he used that.'

'Well. it's difficult to imagine but I don't think I want to comment. You have your own ways of dealing with things in the States, but I think he is probably better off dead. There is one thing, though... Who killed him?'

'Ron Angel.' There was law and there was justice. Doomsday had arrived for Knowles. What a strange and violent land, where a man can dream of fame at any price, and pay that price. I remembered the feeling of pity I had felt for the lonely young man who wanted above all to leave a mark on life. He had achieved his ambition; he would be remembered.

The next day, 19 December, the *Palm Beach Post* reported a press conference held by Yavitz and Rubin after they had heard of

Knowles's death. The newspaper reported Yavitz as saying that he had warned Knowles among other things that certain unnamed police officers had informed him that Knowles's life could be in danger.

'I received such a statement of information from various police officials,' Yavitz is reported as saying. Yavitz also, according to the *Post,* advised Knowles not to try to escape. 'He understood that and I think therefore he was a model prisoner. He never, under any circumstances that I know of, attempted to evoke or create any hostile or potentially hostile environment where he could be shot or injured,' Yavitz is reported as saying. The attorneys are also reported as saying that Knowles had been drugged while in custody.

'Knowles's actions in the last week indicate he was not in a normal state of mind,' Rubin allegedly told reporters. An astonishing comment considering he had killed at least 18 people in four months. At the inquest the jury of four men and one woman listened attentively to the evidence before them. According to the Associated Press report of the inquest, Douglas County Sheriff Earl Lee and GBI agent Ron Angel were transporting Knowles to Henry County where he had promised to show them the location of Campbell's revolver. The two lawmen, using Sheriff Lee's private car, sat in the front; Knowles, handcuffed and in leg irons, was alone in the back.

'Suddenly, over my right shoulder, I felt his body, I saw his face, too,' said Lee, who had been driving the car. 'He went for my gun. We fired my gun. I don't know who fired it, Knowles or me. I shot, Angel shot, I lost control of the car and we wrecked.' Ron Angel gave evidence that he had fired three shots into Knowles as the car careered off the road.

'Knowles was standing as much as possible and bending over the front seat when I began firing.' Knowles had been shot twice in the chest and once in the temple. His death was instant, unlike many of his victims. The assistant director of the State Crime Laboratory testified that one of Knowles's handcuffs was unfastened and dangling from his arm when he examined the body. A bent paperclip was found beneath the corpse. The coroner's jury ruled that the shooting of Paul John Knowles was justifiable self-defence. Despite his forbiddingly military appearance and brooding hostility, Ron Angel was not the trigger-happy cop of film and television. This was his first-ever killing.

When Knowles had stood outside the court after his arraignment for the Carr murders and said to reporters, 'The tapes are what it's all about,' he was right. They continued to be the centre of controversy. A three-judge panel of the Fifth Circuit Court of Appeals – the same power that had released Yavitz from custody – ordered them to be handed over to a federal grand jury in Macon. Yavitz's and Rubin's original arguments were turned skilfully against them. 'Since Knowles is now deceased there is no longer any risk of self-incrimination,' declared the judges.

Early in January, a federal grand jury of 20 people listened to the tapes for five and half hours. Judge Wilbur Owens cautioned them that they were never to disclose the contents. I imagine a caution was all they needed. Owens also released written portions of the transcript to various law enforcement agencies in whose territory crimes had been committed. His attitude to the two Miami attorneys was unchanged by the fact of Knowles's death. Yavitz and Knowles's estate would receive 'only a written deposition of the tapes and nothing else'. This was his final word. A deposition is an opinion or statement of the evidence given by a witness, not a copy of that evidence. Within a week, however, a list had emerged from undisclosed sources; two weeks later the full lurid story was out.

Knowles had indeed driven all over the US in four months. Stolen credit cards documented a journey of approximately 20,000 miles. The trail of murders had begun with a barroom brawl in Jacksonville soon after his return from San Francisco. One night in July, he knifed a bartender and was charged with assault. He spent the night in the slammer at Jacksonville Beach. His futile dreams of going straight had disappeared. But his luck was in and lots of people's was out that night: when no one was watching he kicked his way out of the detention cage and made his escape. On 27 July, in Jacksonville Beach, he broke into the home of Mrs Alice Curtis, 65, a retired schoolteacher who lived on her own. She was found choked to death on her own dentures. She had been bound and robbed and her car, a white Dodge, had been stolen.

On 1 August, in Jacksonville, he kidnapped two little girls from their home when their mother was called away to attend to a sick relative. The bodies of Mylette Josephine Anderson, aged seven, and her sister Lillian Annette, eleven, were found buried in a swamp in January. Their mother was a friend of Knowles's family. The next day, 2 August, in Atlantic Beach, Florida, Mrs Marjorie Howie, 49, was found strangled, a knotted nylon stocking around her neck, another down her throat. Her portable television had been stolen.

On the evening of 23 August, in Musella, Georgia, Mrs Kathy Sue Pierce was strangled with her own telephone cord in the bathroom of her home. Her three-year-old son witnessed the killing but was unharmed. Sometime in August, near Macon, Georgia, an unknown teenage hitchhiker was raped and strangled.

On 3 September, near Lima, Ohio, William Bates, 32, met Knowles in Scott's Inn. His nude body was found bound and strangled in the woods three months after his disappearance. His car, a white Chevrolet, was stolen. Alice Curtis' Dodge was found in the vicinity. From Lima Knowles drove west to Sacramento, California. From there he went north to Seattle, back east to Missoula, Montana, and south into Utah. 12 September found him in Ely, Nevada. Six days later the bodies of Emmett and Lois Johnson, an elderly couple on vacation in a camper, were found. They had been tied up and both had been shot behind the left ear. Their credit cards were missing.

On 23 September, Mrs Charlynn Hicks, a widow aged 42 from Houston, Texas, stopped to admire the view on her way to a chili-cooking contest. Four days later, her body was found. She had been raped, strangled with her tights and dragged through a barbed wire fence. In September or early October, Mrs Anne Dawson, 49, from Birmingham, Alabama, disappeared. She was last seen with a tall, red-haired young man. Her body was never found but is believed to have been dumped in Mississippi.

On 16 October, in Marlborough, Connecticut, Karen White, 35 and her daughter Dawn, 16, were killed. Both had been bound, raped and strangled with knotted nylon stockings. Their bodies were discovered by Mrs White's older daughter, Charyl, a few hours later. Missing from their home was an old-fashioned tape-recorder and a small religious statue of no value.

Knowles then headed south. On 18 October, he arrived in Woodford, Virginia and knocked on the door of a house. It was opened by Mrs Doris Bruce Hovey, 53, and he barged in. Mrs Hovey was shot through the head with a rifle from her husband's study.

Fourteen random victims and perhaps there were many more. Each one of them had met Knowles by chance; each one of them had made one devastating decision. To stay at home rather than go out, to have a drink on the way home, to open the door without checking, to stop and admire the view. None of them had known that their decision was taking them irrevocably towards their fate. Paul John Knowles.

At the inquest, Sheriff Lee had stated that Knowles had drawn the figure 18 on the palm of his left hand when asked how many people he had killed. Adding Carswell and Mandy Carr, Charles Campbell and James Meyer to the 14 murders described in the tapes, that number is the nearest thing to an official total. No one will ever know if he also killed the hitchhikers Edward Hillard and Debbie Griffin. Debbie's body was finally found the August after Knowles died.

Charles Marchman, a Macon lawyer also handling the case for Knowles, said Knowles had once claimed to have killed 35 people, including three in San Francisco the night Angela Covic jilted him. It may have been a ploy for greater glory – according to Marchman he became very depressed as his name slid off the front page – but it could be true. Yavitz told a reporter that Knowles remembered very little about his victims, but he could recall all their possessions. The car he stole from William Bates he loved as his own, caring for it, polishing it, changing the tyres. The victims were shadows to him, characterised in his mind only by the differing ways he killed them.

By the time the list of his victims was published, Knowles had been lying in a Jacksonville cemetery for a month, buried without his heart and lungs which had been unavailable for the drug tests his lawyers had demanded. Angela Covic, the girl he had hoped to marry six short months before, was at the graveside when he was buried.

'I felt fear,' she had said, when asked why she had sent him away after four days. 'Now I think he wanted to include me in his trip, like a Bonnie and Clyde thing.' The Baptist minister conducting the funeral service refused to say the words 'And may his soul rest in peace' over the grave of Paul John Knowles.

It is difficult to not to be sickened and appalled by the long list of useless killings committed by this man, but as the months went by I found it equally difficult to be totally condemning.

Three women had loved Paul John Knowles. His mother, for whom he had such a passionate love that he went out and killed to make her rich and for whom finally, I suppose, he gave his own life. Jackie Knight, who knew his faults and weaknesses but stood by him staunchly. And Angela Covic, his last chance.

Where had that strange, obsessive ambition come from in his 28th year? There was no explorative autopsy to see if a brain tumour could have changed the indolent drifter into the vicious murderer he became. Can a personality change overnight? Do some personalities have a physiological San Andreas Fault built into them so that when the time comes they will split asunder and wreak havoc all around them? Or was it a slow banking-up of emotions, circumstances and bad luck that turned deep, chronic depression into manic aggression?

During the months that followed his death, I learned a little of Knowles's life. He had been institutionalised from the age of eight. A stolen bicycle had led him to a lifetime of foster homes, reformatories and prison. A grey life for a child, a life of uniforms, discipline and few possessions and, like many others going through the system, he learned to live the harsh way, to lie, cheat and steal. And all the while to dream of glory, easy money and escape.

His first prison sentences were for petty thieving and car theft. It was while he was driving a stolen car that he committed his first serious crime. Stopped by a policeman, he grabbed the officer's gun and kidnapped him, letting him go unharmed after two hours. For this he was given five years, a sentence he considered unjust. Perhaps this was the turning-point, the sentence that hardened adolescent bitterness into rage. During years when American youth decried the sanctity of possessions, Knowles was living a brutalised life in prison. There was agitation for gay rights: where Knowles was there was no choice, it was homosexuality or nothing.

Knowles lived his short life with barely a glimpse of the much advertised joys of American living. During the last ten years of his life he was in prison for an average of seven months each year. For stealing an object that was designed to be obsolete within two years he was deprived of freedom, loving relationships and a chance to grow. He was intelligent, with an IQ of 129, but in the ten years he was in and out of jail he never once saw a psychiatrist. Millions of dollars exchange hands in the endless American search for self-fulfilment, yet the ones who need real help receive nothing.

Paul John Knowles was a dreamer. He dreamed of escaping his environment. Sheldon Yavitz later told a reporter that Knowles would have liked to have been a hitman, a hired killer. Such a job would have provided him with the passport to universal acceptance: money. He would have been welcome everywhere, posh nightclubs, restaurants, expensive shops; all the places from which he was excluded.

As it was, no-one recognised the ambitious dreamer within the recalcitrant youth. They trained him to be a welder, so he could return to his own class and be a 'useful member of society'. William B Saxbe reluctantly changed his mind about the possibility of rehabilitation, but he and the society he represents are not prepared to spend more of its resources, mental and material, on improving conditions in the vast impersonal prisons stretched across America. Being treated like shit for years, being fed on an average budget of a few dollars a day, living a life that is often subhuman, is no preparation for becoming a worthwhile human being. Rather, it is fertile breeding ground for that most deadly of emotions: revenge.

Knowles's first known killing was an accident committed during the course of a burglary, but it must have released the rage and fear accumulated over 20 years of isolation and humiliation. His studies of astrology and the tarot cards may even have led him to believe he was doomed, but I believe that in that first killing, looking down at the old lady's corpse, he sensed his own power for the first time in his life. The man who had always been the victim, dominated by judges, juries and jailers, had found revenge, a source of emotional satisfaction.

His attempts at love had all failed him. His mother, Bonnie Knowles, whom he adored, had allowed his father to send him away; the love affairs conducted by mail with Jackie and Angela were both childish and swaggering, the letters filled with sexual boasts. 'There are only two things that I like to do on a rainy day,' he had written to Angela, 'Sleep and Make Love! And I very seldom get sleepy!!!' The lined paper was smothered with kisses, the envelopes with crayonned drawings. Nothing came of these relationships because they were based on fantasy.

He had no experience of living in the everyday world. No wonder the story of Jonathan Livingston Seagull made such an impression on him, he had been an outsider all his life. During his years in prison Knowles would have become familiar with the criminal hierarchy. As a petty thief he would have been somewhere near the bottom of the scale; as a cop kidnapper he may have gained a little respect, though the chances are that someone said: 'You should have killed the bastard!' He would have learned that the killer is the top of the pile. Now he was one. Perhaps that was the moment he decided to be the biggest one of all. He had nothing to lose, the people outside meant nothing to him, the only contact he ever had with them was as they sat in the jury box pronouncing him guilty.

So he embarked on his journey, a 20,000 mile roundtrip on which he saw the vast grandeur of America. Perhaps he wondered why, when there was so much, he had so little. After his capture he told his lawyer he had never let his victims know their fate beforehand. He charmed them into acquiescence by telling them he must tie them up in order to get away. 'I never wanted to hurt them,' he said. He could not understand their terror, and when he killed them he felt no remorse.

In his book *The Murdering Mind*, Dr David Abrahamsen states: 'It is well known that every man who kills, first wanted to kill himself. To the psychiatrist murder is the suicide of the self, however unconscious it may be.' Knowles's behaviour on that last weekend of freedom certainly bears out the theory. He made straight for Georgia, the scene of most of his crimes, the place where death was almost certainly waiting for him,

It is doubtful whether the contents of the tapes will ever be published. They are still in the possession of the grand jury. It is understood that one side is devoted to accounts of the killings, the other to Knowles's opinion of the prison system. It would be too romantic to consider his murder spree as a one-man Attica, desperately trying to attract the world's attention to the plight of the people behind bars, but perhaps one day the transcripts will be circulated amongst prison administrators, psychiatrists and legislators. Someone somewhere might even learn how to avoid turning an eight-year-old bicycle thief into a major criminal.

As I researched Knowles's background I began to understand our journey: the long silences filled with images of death; the significance of that sad and haunting tune of John Denver's that he always turned to full volume; the intimate sharing of my past, which, of course, he understood, it was so similar to his own; the curious sympathy between us. I think there were two main reasons for my survival. To him I meant publicity, the fame he craved. Then for a week I helped him create his *alter ego*, Daryl Golden, the man he wanted to be, could have been, perhaps. Through my merciful ignorance he was able, just for a week, to live his own American dream. For a week he was a nice, middle-class young man with a car, credit cards and a girl of his own; a man accepted by society, well-mannered, well-dressed. In that week he found kindness, warmth, laughter and fun. Perhaps, for the first time, he began to see what life could have been like. But of course it was already too late.

I will never know for certain whether he would have killed me that last night, the one when I said goodbye so determinedly. His pattern was to kill approximately every ten days and he fulfilled it at the weekend. As it is, my instinct for survival was stronger than his. I am sure that when I arrived at that darkened bar in Atlanta, obviously alone and nervous, I was the next potential victim. I turned out to be the catalyst; it was my knowledge of the existence of the tapes that led to his death. I was his karma.

Two people, both outcasts, both raised by the State, one from the Old World, the other from the New. One given every opportunity to develop as a human being, the other growing up an outlaw in the land of equal opportunity for all. One growing to achievement in a class-ridden society, the other treated worse than a dog in a country that glories in its classlessness. It is difficult not to draw conclusions. All I know is that in that week I met the man buried deep within the institutionalised monster who shocked the world, and with that knowledge peace has returned to me.

Paul John Knowles was as much a victim as any of the 18 people he killed. With a compassion that in no way diminishes my sorrow for the dead and my sympathy for those who mourn them, I find I cannot share the uncharitable attitude of that Baptist minister.

May his poor, demented soul rest in peace.

Afterword,
February 2004,
London

FOUR MONTHS IN 1974 TURNED PAUL JOHN KNOWLES FROM A HANDSOME FLORIDA PETTY THIEF INTO ONE OF THE MOST FEARED MEN IN AMERICA. Roaming throughout the country in a series of cars stolen from his victims, he committed brutal murders and became a modern nightmare. The criminological term for his kind had not been coined back in the mid-1970s, but is all too familiar now: a serial killer.

After his arrest Knowles claimed a tally of 35 victims: the most widely accepted 'probable' total is 20. The additional deaths were those of two young hitchhikers, Edward Hilliard and Debbie Griffin. They were killed on or shortly before 5 November, 1974. Early on 6 November, he murdered Carswell Carr and raped and murdered his 15 year-old daughter, Mandy. The following evening I met Knowles in the bar of an Atlanta hotel.

The prime reason why I wrote this account is as clear now as it was 30 years ago: I had to find out what could have made a human being suddenly do such inhuman things. How could the charming if gauche Daryl Golden I met in the Holiday Inn really be the serial killer Paul John Knowles? I felt he had befouled me irrevocably and I hated myself for being associated with him.

Partly my reaction was due to my shame that he had been able to deceive me of all people, a self-reliant, hard-bitten, woman who reckoned the knocks of early life and working in journalism enabled her to see through any man, at work or in the bedroom. Partly it was the dreadful sense that I may have been incredibly lucky to be able to tell my tale. Another woman who travelled with him for six days was not.

Ann Dawson, a beautician who fell for his good looks and enthrallingly deep voice in Birmingham, Alabama, paid for their excursion until he bored of the game, killed her and hid her body. It has never been found. The suspicion that I was spared her fate because as a journalist I could tell the public about him once his deeds became known appalled me. The alternative, that I was not killed because I escaped before he decided to strike, was no better. Contemplating either reason sickened me as much as the memory of his touch.

That is still how I feel. He haunts me and re-reading this book I realise that I hid much of my fear and self-loathing behind the journalistic impulse to report the facts and through them detect an answer.

Whether I even came close is for a reader to decide. My suspicion remains that when Knowles realised that he had killed the retired schoolteacher Alice Curtis in the course of a burglary he suddenly felt a power over his fellow beings he had never experienced before. Deprived of human respect in the institutions that dominated his life from the age of eight, he became addicted to a despicable way of tearing it from people.

Accounts he gave his lawyers and his making tapes about his murders while he was on the road suggest that he saw killing as a way to achieve fame, to stand out at last. If so, Paul John Knowles was far from the last man to seek infamy because some flaw means he cannot win its nobler twin, fame. Perversely, he may have thought his murders would make his mother rich and proud of him because she would be able to sell his history and his tapes after he was dead.

Those tapes may provide a fuller answer to his motivation but I no longer wish to hear them. Ironically, it will soon be possible to do so for the first time. At the end of the January 1975 hearing described in this book, Judge Owens ruled that they be sealed for 30 years. That order runs out in just a few months from now.

Sheldon Yavitz, the Miami lawyer whose refusal to surrender the tapes to the Georgia authorities led to his being imprisoned until a federal appeal court released him, later received a felony conviction for tax fraud. It has not proved so easy to update the stories of other people who feature in this book, such as Angela Covic, who broke off her engagement to Knowles shortly before he commenced his killing spree and agent Ron Angel who shot him. However I can write about what happened to me since 1974.

Thirty years is a long time in anyone's life. I am no longer the carefree, energetic, young woman who wrote this account.

Indeed, I realised that I had changed not long after I returned to London and Fleet Street. So had the way people regarded me. In a few weeks I had gone from admired golden girl who covered wars to sullied scarlet woman.

The notoriety of my connection with a killer gave my new editor on the *Daily Express* an excuse to be rid of me and I was offered redundancy as a blunt alternative to the sack. I took it and used the money and time it allowed me to start this book but I never had a staff job on a newspaper again.

In a way I outlived the environment I had been asked to leave. I freelanced for almost another 20 years, long after Fleet Street itself was no more. The major newspapers are now scattered across London from Docklands to Kensington. Not one thrums to the sound of hot metal presses starting their run in the evening, a noise that always quickened my pulse. You do not see journalists in the City Golfing Club or the countless other drinking holes between Ludgate Circus and the Strand. They are not even to be seen having a lunchtime sharpener between assignments near their sterile new offices. The raucous profession I loved has become as staid and establishment as banking.

At the time being made redundant by the *Express* seemed unfair but, given the cutbacks the business consultants were imposing on the paper and the new broom's dislike of me, at least it was foreseeable. The same could not be said of the salacious way a goodly number of my male colleagues viewed my experiences. They conflated sex and violence and were excited by the cocktail of the two that Knowles had created.

This nauseated me. Violent sex is a painful part of many people's intimate relationships, usually fuelled by jealousy, inadequacy or booze, but raping a random woman while you kill her is a far darker problem. Their inability to see that and their treatment of it as a turn-on changed my attitude to men.

Not completely, though. Over the years I enjoyed several more lovers, wrote several more books and had quite a few more drinks. Thirty years on my eyesight is no longer strong enough to spot a good-looking man at the end of the bar and my inclinations no longer strong enough to care that I can't. I still have red hair and the gift of the gab, although nowadays the former is thanks to a bottle from Boots the Chemist and I haven't exercised my waspish tongue in print for some years. Those wonderful, wicked days are over, as gone as old Fleet Street, but life goes on. Encountering Paul John Knowles taught me to value that gift all the more.

In a way it was a good thing that he died, killed on a road as many of his victims were. Had Knowles spent years rotting on Death Row I would have written to him, still desperate to understand why. I was younger then.

Now I am not sure that I am as keen to find some streak in him deserving of sympathy, some explanation going even a little way towards exculpating him or making others share the blame. He and I had the bond of being outsiders as children but then so was the teenage girl he raped and strangled for amusement some time that August. No one ever claimed her, not a parent, sibling or lover. She remains known only by the bland cipher American law uses for unidentified women and legal fictions: Jane Doe. Whatever that poor girl's real name, another soul alone in the world, she deserved better from life than to meet Paul John Knowles.

The kindness I received from relatives of his victims after this book first came out further emphasised how lucky I was simply to be alive. Members of Trooper Charles Campbell's family and the mother of teenage hitchhiker Debbie Griffin contacted me and said that reading it had helped them understand why someone they loved had been cold-bloodedly murdered. Their kind words and sentiments were an enormous comfort to me. Nothing I can say can remove sorrow such as theirs but I hope that the years have treated them and all the other families kindly.

Good friends brighten anyone's life and I have been blessed with the companionship of more than my fair share of excellent examples. Inevitably some of the closest have died over the last three decades but I am fortunate to still have the company of many.

As what used to be called a foundling and having been brought up in orphanages, a family of my own is an incredible joy. My three remarkable children, Jo, Kate and Jamie, continue to be a source of happiness and pride to me but the best change that has happened in the last 30 years is that now I have two lovely grandchildren. Every time I see Leah and Flynn they remind me how lucky I am to have enjoyed the gift of life to the full. In gratitude for that, I dedicate this republishing to them.

Sandy Fawkes, London, 2004